WHEN GOD MET A GIRL

WHEN GOD MET A GIRL

Life-Changing Encounters with Women of the Bible

ANDREW SNADEN

LIFE JOURNEY®
Bringing Home the Message for Life

COOK COMMUNICATIONS MINISTRIES
Colorado Springs, Colorado • Paris, Ontario
KINGSWAY COMMUNICATIONS LTD
Eastbourne, England

Life Journey® is an imprint of
Cook Communications Ministries, Colorado Springs, CO 80918
Cook Communications, Paris, Ontario
Kingsway Communications, Eastbourne, England

WHEN GOD MET A GIRL

First Printing, 2007
Printed in the United States of America
1 2 3 4 5 6 7 8 9 10

Cover Design: Jeffrey P. Barnes
Cover Photo: BigStock Photo

ISBN 978-0-7814-4433-0
LCCN 2006932570

To the three girls in my life:
my mom, my wife, my daughter.
With all my love, Andrew Snaden

CONTENTS

ACKNOWLEDGMENTS

I'd like to thank some people for their assistance with this book:

To Mike Nappa, whose help and input were invaluable.

To Pastor Ellis Wedel, for being willing to answer questions like: "Could this have happened?" "Why do you think they did that?" and many others.

To Diane Gardner, for editing this book and providing great suggestions.

To my wife, for being a good listener.

To my readers, for letting me share part of my life with them.

And to Jesus of Nazareth—God who met a girl. After writing this book, I finally get it.

INTRODUCTION

The boys stood in a line facing the girls, and a recipe for disaster was written. That day in physical education class we were going to learn to dance—and the girl who faced you would be your partner.

It became like a game of musical chairs without the chairs. Twelve fifteen-year-old boys jockeyed for position to avoid facing Shelley (not her real name).

Shelley was one of those girls to whom puberty gave its every curse and none of its blessings. Puberty gave her the oily, stringy hair and a face ravaged with acne that no cream could treat, but none of the curves the other girls got. She endured ridicule from both sides.

Whichever boy got stuck dancing with Shelley would suffer mocking and scorn from the other guys. If it weren't so cruel, it would've been funny watching us guys pushing each other to avoid being across from her.

The teacher lost patience with us and demanded we settle down and someone dance with her or else. We all chose or else.

So no one learned to dance that day. Instead, we sat on the floor while the teacher took a weeping Shelley to the school nurse for comfort.

Honestly, if I could go back in time and undo that moment, I would. I'd dance with Shelley, and I wouldn't care what the other guys thought. But I can't go back in time. All I can do is tell the Shelleys of this world something I've learned.

There's a whole culture lined up against you and— no matter how plain or pretty you are—it will always find some way to tear you down. Like a bunch of immature, giggling boys elbowing each other, it seeks opportunity to send you to the school nurse in tears.

Well, you don't have to run crying to the nurse when you need encouragement. You get to run to the creator of the universe—Jesus. You get to run to the one who can not only dry your tears but also build you up, so the next time you face the challenges of life, you can hold your head up and overcome them because you know he who loves you is the only one who matters. And you matter to him, too.

God met a lot of girls during his earthly ministry, and he showed them how much he cared.

God met a girl caught in adultery—and forgave her. God met a girl who suffered from chronic bleeding— and healed her. God met a girl who lost her only son—and brought him back from the dead. Jesus met young women, he met old women, and he met sick women. He treated them all the same; he loved them all the same.

Jesus wants to meet you. My hope and prayer is that as you turn the pages of this book, you'll read the events of that love and let that love shield you from the harshness of the times we live in. I pray that after you read this book you can boldly say, "I met God, and I know he loves me."

Author's note: To make it easy for you to follow, any fictionalized accounts appear in Futura CondensedLight font without the gray background set off by the woman's eyes graphic (which are direct Scripture quotations). Within those sections, I've remained true to the Bible, including any conversations Scripture records.

1

A WOMAN CAUGHT IN ADULTERY

(GRACE)

The door banged open.

Her eyes flashed from lust to fear. Angry hands reached from behind, grabbing at her shoulders and pulling her away from me. Two large men held her between them while two more crowded into the small room. The eldest of the group, Simeon, spat on her.

"Harlot," he said.

She looked at me like a frightened child, hoping I could do something. Anything. The men also looked at me, smirking. I rose from the bed, slowly wrapping a sheepskin around myself. I measured each man carefully before turning to her, then I spat on her myself.

Her eyes searched mine. "I . . . I don't understand."

Simeon stepped around and faced her. "You don't need to understand. All you need to know is you've been caught committing adultery. All you need to know is the law requires you to be stoned to death."

Her eyes looked to me, then back at Simeon. "No, that can't be."

"It can and it is," he said. The big men released her as Simeon grabbed her hair and pulled her toward the door. She looked back at me, frightened. Betrayed. "But what about him?"

Simeon paused, looked at me, and grunted. "What about him? He's done nothing wrong." Another of the men grabbed her and, with Simeon, pulled her from the room kicking and screaming. I picked my robe up off the floor, put it on, and followed them into the dry, dusty street.

Priests and scribes were waiting in the street, shouting and reviling the woman. Her pleadings fell on deaf ears as they dragged her toward the temple. The sharp little rocks embedded in the dirt road slashed at her bare feet. Eventually she lost her balance and the cuts appeared on her body. It wouldn't be long before rocks the size of fists crushed her to death. They just needed her for one more task, and then they could get it over with.

The little mob had neared the temple when a patrol of Roman soldiers blocked their path. A horse-mounted centurion looked down at the mob. His eyebrows lifted at the sight of the naked and bleeding woman.

"What's going on here?" he said.

Simeon stepped forward. "We caught this woman committing adultery. We're taking her to be stoned as it says in the law."

The centurion looked down at the woman, his face impassive, and then turned his attention to Simeon. "You're under Roman law. No one gets put to death without Roman consent."

"Then consent," Simeon said. "She's a harlot." He moved a little closer to the centurion. "Unless there's some reason you wish to protect her?"

The centurion's eyes shifted for a second. "There has to be a trial."

"There will be," Simeon said. "Jesus the great teacher is in town. We will have him judge her."

A slight grin flitted across the centurion's face. "You will have Jesus judge her?"

"Yes."

"And you'll accept his judgment?"

"Of course." It was Simeon's turn to grin.

The centurion leaned back on his horse and gently moved the reins. The horse backed away from the center of the street; the centurion's men followed suit. "Then you may go."

The crowd started to move.

"Wait!" The centurion held his hand up.

The crowd staggered to a stop.

"Yes," Simeon said.

"Where's the man she committed adultery with?"

My stomach roiled and my heart hammered. We had a deal, and it didn't include rocks bouncing off of my head. The woman started to turn — to look back at me, to point at me? One of the men grabbed her shoulder, and she winced in pain. She kept her eyes toward the ground.

"Oh, he ran away," Simeon said.

My heart started to settle down.

"Didn't she run?" the centurion said.

"What does that have to do with anything?" Simeon said.

"Well, if he ran, she ran. How come you only caught her?"

"He was very fast," Simeon said.

The centurion rubbed his chin. "I see. Tell me, what did he look like?"

Simeon tilted his head and my heart started to hammer again. "What he looked like?"

"Yes," the centurion said. "What did the man who got away look like?"

"Why?"

The centurion grinned. "We'll help you find him. Surely you'll want to bring both of them to justice."

Simeon glanced over at me and my knees almost buckled. "We didn't get a good look at him. We only saw his back."

"Of course you did," the centurion said. He unfastened his cloak and flung it toward Simeon. "At least cover her with this."

Simeon picked up the cloak and tossed it to the woman, who quickly wrapped it around herself. He looked up at the centurion. "Compassion? From a Roman? I've seen it all now."

The centurion smirked. "The day is young." He backed his horse out of their way.

It didn't take the mob long to work itself back into indignant rage as they dragged my "lover" to the temple. They burst through the temple entrance, and people inside quickly parted to make way for the priests and scribes. At the center sat the so-called prophet Jesus; now they'd prove he was nothing but a deceiver. He claimed to be the Son of God. Word was that Jesus was going around eating with and forgiving sinners. Only God could forgive sins, and if Jesus forgave this woman, they'd have him. And if he didn't, well, one less adulteress in town.

Someone gave the woman a hard shove, and she collapsed, trembling in front of Jesus.

"Teacher," Simeon said with mock respect, "this woman was caught in adultery, *in the very act.* Now Moses, in the law, commanded us that such should be stoned." Simeon paused, setting his trap and enjoying it. Finally, he continued, "But what do you say?"

I kept to the back of the priests and scribes, standing at an angle so I'd be out of the woman's sight. But it didn't matter. She never looked up anyway. She just lay there, sobbing silently, awaiting death.

A stillness settled over the temple. A nervous shuffling moved through the priests and scribes, and they started to demand that he answer them. Jesus stood up and locked his eyes on Simeon's. He said it quietly, without a hint of emotion, but the challenge was fierce nonetheless.

"He who is without sin among you, let him throw a stone at her first."

No one moved, no one breathed. It seemed as if time had stopped, just for this moment, just for this man. Just for this . . . ?

Suddenly, Jesus stooped down and began writing on the ground. I couldn't see what he wrote, but Simeon could. He turned, his face ashen, and walked past us all. In turn by age, all the priests and scribes, their faces drained of color, left.

I didn't have to fear the woman accusing me. Her eyes were on Jesus, tears streaming down her face. I stepped forward, looked at what he wrote, what he wrote for all to see. He'd written about me. Why had the priests and scribes just walked past me? With what Jesus wrote, they couldn't let me live.

I retreated to the back of the temple, waiting for the crowd to

But Jesus went to the Mount of Olives.

Now early in the morning He came again into the temple, and all the people came to Him; and He sat down and taught them. Then the scribes and Pharisees brought to Him a woman caught in adultery. And when they had set her in the midst, they said to Him, "Teacher, this woman was caught in adultery, in the very act. Now Moses, in the law, commanded us that such should be stoned. But what do You say?" This they said, testing Him, that they might have *something* of which to accuse Him. But Jesus stooped down and wrote on the ground with *His* finger, as though He did not hear.

So when they continued asking Him, He raised Himself up and said to them, "He who is without sin among you, let him throw a stone at her first." And again He stooped down and wrote on the ground. Then those who heard *it*, being convicted by *their* conscience, went out one by one, beginning with the oldest *even* to the last. And Jesus was left alone, and the woman standing in the midst. When Jesus had raised Himself up and saw no one but the woman, He said to her, "Woman, where are those accusers of yours? Has no one condemned you?"

She said, "No one, Lord."

And Jesus said to her, "Neither do I condemn you; go and sin no more."

Then Jesus spoke to them again, saying, "I am the light of the world. He who follows Me shall not walk in darkness, but have the light of life." (John 8:1–12) turn on me, but they kept their eyes on Jesus. They were waiting to see what he was going to do with the woman.

Jesus rose up and looked at the woman.

"Woman, where are those accusers of yours? Has no one condemned you?"

She said, "No one, Lord."

And Jesus said to her, "Neither do I condemn you; go and sin no more."

The crowd began to murmur. He was actually going to let her go. Jesus turned to them. "I am the light of the world. He who follows Me shall not walk in darkness, but have the light of life." (Dialogue taken from John 8:4–12.)

One of my college instructors told the story of a divisional accountant who made an error that cost a multinational corporation more than a million dollars. He was "summoned" to the head office to meet with the president and vice president.

My instructor said he looked like he was going to an execution. His shoulders were stooped, his walk slow, his head hanging low. Not only was he going to be fired, but his professional reputation was effectively ruined as well. After that meeting, this guy's next job would probably include saying, "Would you like fries with that?"

My instructor—who was one of the home-office accountants at the time—said the guy went into the president's office and the meeting lasted less than a minute. When he came out, he looked stunned. My instructor asked what happened.

He said, "I opened the door and they both looked at me. Charlie (the president) asked, 'Do you know what you did wrong?'

"I said yes.

"'Do you think you'll ever do it again?'

"I said no.

"Charlie said, 'Well, there's no point in firing you, because the next guy will probably make the same mistake. Go back to work.'"

Imagine the intense relief he felt! He knew he deserved to be fired, and suddenly it was as if nothing had ever happened. He wouldn't have to sell his home, give up his golf membership, and return his Lexus.

The woman in the story at the beginning of this chapter—commonly known to history as "the woman caught in adultery"—must have felt something even more intense. She had no reason to believe she'd escape punishment just because her accusers had left. There was a law that demanded she be put to death. If Jesus were a prophet, he would follow the law.

Of course, she probably didn't know this at the time, but Jesus is more than a prophet, more than the law. He is God! And he did follow the law. The law says,

> Whoever is deserving of death shall be put to death on the testimony of two or three witnesses; he shall not be put to death on the testimony of one witness. (Deut. 17:6)

After Jesus fingered that mysterious writing on the ground, the witnesses disappeared, almost like evaporating smoke. For some reason, they just didn't feel like testifying anymore, and without them, this bleeding woman couldn't be put to death.

Now, why did Jesus let her off? She wasn't a nice person. She ran a little business somewhere near town that contributed to the society's moral decay. Jesus could've kept his finger off the ground, let them accuse her, pronounced sentence, and let the rocks fly.

The rocks didn't fly because of one simple word with fathomless meaning:

Grace.

The dictionary defines *grace* as "the free and unmerited favor or beneficence of God." Do you know what that meant for the woman caught in adultery? Simply this: Jesus let her off because he felt like it. There was nothing she did or could have done to earn that break. The God who became man chose not to condemn her.

She must have been one confused girl. The people who were guilty condemned her, and the one who was guiltless forgave her. She must have felt like that guy who fully expected to be fired, only to return to his old job.

The big difference here, though, is I doubt she ever returned to her old job. How could she? She'd met the light of the world; she'd experienced true saving grace firsthand; she was changed. So changed, in fact, that I've taken to calling her something other than "the woman caught in adultery." I've grown fond of calling her by the name that describes how Christ treated her, the name that reminds me how I should treat others like her—like me.

Grace.

And so our wounded, broken Grace looked up and found freedom in the eyes of God, found joy in the face of the Savior, lost her life and found it again in the hands of the one who dared defend her when she deserved only death.

What about those guilty guys and their rocks?

No one knows for sure what Jesus actually scribbled in the dirt during this encounter, but whatever it was, it had a momentous effect on the priests and scribes. One minute they were lusting for the blood of a helpless, beaten woman. The next, the most they could muster was a meek and hasty retreat from God's presence.

And why was it so easy for them to condemn this woman to death?

During the time of Christ, stoning had to be right up there with crucifixion as a brutal form of execution, yet these so-called religious leaders had no problem with it. In fact, they were eager to spill the woman's blood, to crush her body into a disfigured shell of flesh. How could they be so "holy," and yet so bloodthirsty and cruel?

It's easy to kill what you don't know, but nearly impossible to kill what you love.

I once owned a horse that had to be put down, and I just couldn't shoot it, even though that was the right thing to do. Instead, I called my local vet and she did the deed for me. To her it was just another horse that needed to be euthanized. To me it wasn't just a horse; it was a friend—my companion and riding buddy, not an object.

So how did these religious men get to the point where they could, like that veterinarian, view Grace as simply another "horse" that needed to be euthanized? How could they actually *look forward* to the prospect of brutally killing her? Sure, the whole point of the exercise appears to have been a way to trap Jesus, but I believe they were counting on him having to go with the law. Once Jesus did that, I'm certain they would've been pressing a rock in his hand and making him join in.

The Scriptures don't actually say what this woman did for a living, but it seems to me if they needed a woman to catch in adultery on short notice, she would have to be a prostitute. So they found one, and what these men did from that point was remove the woman's humanity. She wasn't a woman in their eyes; she wasn't a child of God, created in his image and imbued with the beauty of his touch. She was a "harlot." And once her humanity was removed she became merely an object, and stoning an object was something they could do.

And yet ...

That's not what Jesus saw at all. His eyes looked at the same person the would-be killers looked at, but Jesus didn't see just an object or a "harlot."

He saw a woman.

In fact, he saw more than that. He saw the little girl she had been; he saw the twists and turns of life, the choices and desperation that thrust her on that path of life; he saw everything that led her to the moment she stood before him—and beyond. He saw Grace, who—made stainless with his love—would go on to live a new life of grace and hope, and with a passion for more than just satisfying her physical lust. Jesus saw the complete her and loved her as a result. So he did what only God can do. He forgave, and in his forgiving she found new life.

But the Pharisees couldn't do that. Hatred of Jesus consumed them. He was rocking the apple cart, and it didn't matter who died if they could discredit him. And yet Jesus showed them grace too, even though they didn't realize it.

Ever wonder what Jesus wrote in the sand? Well, no one knows, but I have an idea. I want to share it with you by ending the story.

Jesus' words cut right into me. I feared to go outside, but listening to Jesus made me want to scream. His words were like the rocks we were going to throw at the woman.

I stumbled outside the temple and held up my arms, expecting a volley of stones to batter me to death; but the priests and scribes weren't there. Maybe they were somewhere holding a meeting, a mock trial. Then they'd pass a sentence. A death sentence. I had to leave town.

I kept away from the main streets on my way home. I rounded the corner to my street and came face-to-face with Simeon. His face was filled with shame as he looked at me.

"So, now you know," he said.

"Know what?"

"My sins. He showed all of you my sins. How can someone who is supposed to be *just* a man know my darkest deeds and thoughts?"

I went cold. "Jesus wrote your sins in the dirt?"

Simeon nodded slowly.

Now I understood. Jesus had written one thing in the dirt, but we all read it differently. We all read only about our own sins. No man had this ability. Only God could know what Jesus knew.

I turned around and ran toward the temple, hoping Jesus would show me the same mercy he'd shown the woman.

Forgive me for shifting gears here, but stick with me, because it will all make sense in a moment.

Ever change your hairstyle, and all your "friends" lie to you and say it looks nice when it really doesn't? Then you ask your spouse what he or she thinks, and your spouse kind of looks away and says, "Do you want the truth, or a nice lie?"

"The truth, of course," you say. So they tell you the truth, and it hurts, but it beats walking around looking silly. The people who love us will tell us the truth even when it's going to hurt, because we can't get any better if nobody tells us the truth.

Now, even though it doesn't seem like it, Jesus actually extended grace to more than the woman before him; he also gave grace to the men who were craving the death of the sinner they'd brought. These guys had no clue about their own spiritual condition. They felt they were righteous enough to execute a fellow human being, unaware of the depravity of their own souls. And they were slow learners, too. How clear can you make it?

> He who is without sin among you, let him throw a stone at her first. (John 8:7)

That should have been enough to open their eyes to the absurdity of the situation. *They were all guilty of sin, yet they felt righteous enough to condemn this woman* ... a woman who, in all likelihood, they enticed into sin, only to discover they'd entrapped themselves.

So Jesus offered them a glimpse of the truth, writing something on the ground that spoke truth directly into their sin-soaked lives. Whatever it was, it took all the wind out of their sails.

These guys probably didn't appreciate what Jesus wrote, but if they had, they would have found that it was the beginning of their healing, their redemption. He showed them that they, too, dangled on the precipice of God's condemnation. He did this because he loved them, too. For Grace, all it took was a simple "Neither do I condemn you; go and sin no more" (John 8:11).

For the men, it took revealing something so embarrassing they could do nothing but walk away. Too bad they didn't stick around for the last lesson:

> I am the light of the world. He who follows
> Me shall not walk in darkness, but have the
> light of life. (John 8:12)

When I was a teenager I joined the army cadets. It's sort of like army reserve for teenagers. One weekend we were on night maneuvers. The plan was to circle around the "enemy" and attack them from behind. Our sergeant said, "Follow me," and we did.

We followed him through the bush, down a hill, into a stream, and back up the hill, where we proceeded to march right into an ambush, and we all "died" according to the rules of the military-combat game.

Our sergeant didn't mean to get us all killed. *He really believed in what he was doing. He just believed wrong.*

"I am the light of the world. He who follows Me shall not walk in darkness, but have the light of life."

Until their encounter with Jesus, everyone in that temple was walking in darkness. Some, like Grace, chose to begin walking in light. Others chose to follow the "sergeant" of sin deeper into the darkness. Jesus is the only one we can trust to always lead us to safety and bring light into our lives.

And that, my friend, is truly God's grace.

2

A WOMAN WITH AN ISSUE OF BLOOD

(FAITH)

Pain. Every morning pain, along with its sister, discomfort, awoke Leah long before the birds heralded the sunrise. For twelve years now, these two sisters had repeatedly stolen a full night's sleep from her. But this day, Leah thanked them, because this morning she needed to leave before the sun peeked over the horizon.

She eased herself upright and paused a moment to let the dizziness pass. Leah felt around the small table beside her bed and found the bowl of nuts and figs. She chewed slowly, taking sips of water from the adjacent cup of water. Only one physician chose not to try painful treatments on her; that physician told Leah this curse would die with her, but the right food and water could give her some measure of strength.

Next, Leah went through the task of cleaning herself from the night's issue. She kept a bowl of water and cloths near the end of the bed for this purpose. She'd done this ritual so many times that the darkness didn't hinder her.

Her heart jumped when the birds began their symphony; the day's journey would be long. Leah hastily dressed, felt her way to the door, grabbed the sack of food and extra clothing she'd prepared before nightfall, and stepped out into the street.

Already, fingers of sunlight started to paint the canvas of a new day. Fighting through the pain, Leah hurried down the street to the outskirts of the leper colony and started her quest for the man who could banish the two sisters of pain and discomfort forever.

Walking helped ease the cramps, and after about five minutes she settled into an easy pace. Feeling the early morning sun on her face, breathing in the crisp air, a stranger visited her — Hope. This time it would be different. This healer, this Jesus, wouldn't hurt her like the others. A nervous smile of anticipation broke across Leah's face.

"So, you're really going to go to him."

Leah's hands went to her chest as a shape moved from a bush onto the road and blocked her way.

"Sarah, what are you doing here?"

Her older sister stood hands on hips, lips pressed tightly together. "Stopping you from getting your heart broken again."

"Were you out here all night? Don't you know how dangerous the road is?"

Sarah sneered. "Do you know how dangerous a man claiming to be the Son of God is?"

"Jesus isn't dangerous. He's ... he's the Messiah."

Sarah quickly looked behind her. "Don't ever let anyone hear you say that. Father says that's blasphemy."

Leah balled her hands into fists. "Yes, if any man would know the law, it would be Father. The law. If I remember correctly that's the reason he cast me from the house."

Sarah took a deep breath. "Leah, he didn't have any choice. You're unclean."

"That didn't mean he had to throw me out of the house. Father just didn't want to take the chance I'd accidentally touch him and he couldn't go to temple and pretend to be holy with the rest of his friends."

"Leah, be fair. He gave you more than enough money to care for yourself. It isn't his fault you wasted it on so-called physicians. By the way, how much does this Jesus charge?"

"He doesn't charge anything."

"How do you know?"

"A leper from my colony was healed. That's how we learned about Jesus. He never charged that man."

Sarah shook her head. "That's not what Father says. He says this Jesus is making a fortune off of fools."

"And how would Father know that?"

"He's heard things. He has friends in the temple."

"And I've seen a man whose skin was ravaged with leprosy come back without a blemish, and with fingers he lost to disease restored. He told us this Jesus is different. He said when he speaks, your soul pushes at your chest trying to get out and rush to him. If only I can touch him, I know he can heal me."

Sarah clenched her fists. "Leah, how many times have you said 'I heard about this physician, or that physician, and if only I can get to him, I'll be healed.' Don't do this. You'll be brokenhearted for weeks. Just go home and rest."

"Those physicians were just men. Jesus is the M—"

Sarah held up her hand. "No, don't say it again."

Leah took a deep breath and released it slowly. "He is what he is, Sarah. Now please step aside. I've a long journey and not much energy to complete it."

Sarah reached her hand forward. "Give me your bag."

"No, Sarah. I am going to see Jesus."

"I understand, Sister. Give me the bag. Just like all the other times, I'm going to go so that you've got a shoulder to cry on when your heart is broken, and what little money you have left is gone."

Leah handed the bag to her sister. "When this day is over, the only tears we'll share will be tears of joy."

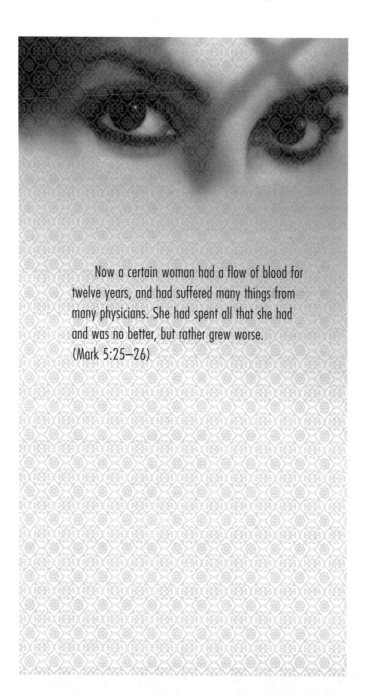

Now a certain woman had a flow of blood for twelve years, and had suffered many things from many physicians. She had spent all that she had and was no better, but rather grew worse.
(Mark 5:25–26)

A woman who experiences menstrual-like bleeding for twelve years ... now there's a natural topic for inclusion in the gospel of Jesus Christ, right? Apparently so, as Mark included this story in his biography of the Son of God.

It's easy to trivialize this woman's problem. She suffered from something all women suffer from—just all the time. But it was more than that. It was more than just the discomfort; it was the social rejection that came with it.

On a superficial level, her plight kind of reminds me of that time back in junior high school (we've all had times like this) when you were in a group of friends and suddenly broke wind (the polite way of saying farted). The sound—just like one of those big "number one" Styrofoam hands fans wave at basketball games—made it clear to everyone around that you were the culprit.

Remember how they all looked at you in disgust, groaning as if they'd never farted themselves? Then those closest to you pinched their noses and scooted quickly away. For that moment, you became Leah—an outcast. A normal bodily function stuck a big, fat label—"stinker"—on your forehead, and the group pushed you away.

You probably just wanted to crawl under a rock and die. Fortunately for you, the smell faded, and the group, well aware that someday it would be their turn, forgot about it and life went on. But for the woman described in this passage, life never "went on."

Leah bore the social penalty of having an illness that made her—and anyone she touched—unclean.[1]

Most certainly, Leah's father turned her out of the house to save his social life. One touch from his daughter and he would be unable to go to temple with the rest of the guys until he went through the cleansing ritual.

Even if he had kept Leah in a separate part of the house, and the family observed strict rules so no one ever touched her, it still wouldn't have been good enough because everyone would know an "unclean" lived in his home. His friends would assume he was unclean. Appearances were everything, and the only way Leah's father could deal with his daughter was to give her some cash and wish her all the best.

So where could she go? Beneath every "for rent" sign there must have been some sort of "no uncleaners" sign. What self-respecting landlord would want an unclean person living in his building? There's no way he'd take the risk of bumping into her in the hallway.

Maybe you're thinking Leah was married. Surely the handsome prince who married her protected Leah from a cruel and judgmental society. Not likely. Not when he could easily get out of the marriage by invoking Deuteronomy 24:1:

> When a man takes a wife and marries her, and it happens that she finds no favor in his eyes because he has found some uncleanness in her, and he writes her a certificate of divorce, puts it in her hand, and sends her out of his house …

The woman I call Leah most likely ended up living with the lepers. The people no one wanted would have been the only ones who took her into their fellowship and care. She might even have had a bearable life in the colony. The cash, whether it came from her father or her husband, provided the little extras.

But Leah couldn't have wanted just a bearable life; she wanted her old life back. She wanted the freedom to love and to touch, the comfort of a good night's sleep, the peace that comes from knowing your body is working as it should. So she used the cash to try to claw her way back into normal society. Somewhere out there, she must have reasoned, someone had to be able to make her well.

The Scriptures don't say exactly what caused the woman to suffer prolonged bleeding, but one thing is clear: She was afflicted with a uniquely female ailment in a male-dominated society. I shudder to think what abuse those ancient physicians likely heaped on Leah. The Bible only tells us she suffered at the hands of these men. My guess is few doctors at the Jerusalem School of Medicine scrambled to take the course on "How to Deal with Women's Complaints."

These "physicians" probably had no clue what Leah suffered from and just tried whatever came into their minds. Those treatments could have ranged from attempting to stop the issue by blocking its escape to cauterization.

Oh, poor Leah! What did you ever do to deserve this?

I can see her standing at the edge of the colony

some starry night, looking upward to heaven, and asking God: Why? Why did he afflict her? Why did he let those doctors nearly cripple her? Why did he fling her from association with other people? Why did he isolate her from those she loved and those who loved her?

How did God encourage Leah to seek his Son out? A woman so abused and brokenhearted surely by now had given up.

Earlier in the book of Mark (1:40–45), Jesus heals a leper and tells him to keep it a secret. But this guy can't keep it a secret. He's out there "proclaiming freely" what happened.

I'm speculating that maybe on that starry night, Leah heard a commotion in the camp. This leper (I'll call him Bob) has returned. But Bob isn't a leper anymore. Bob is healed. Bob tells about Jesus, a man bucking the system, a man who healed a leper and others.

Leah would've pushed through the crowd to see for herself. There stood Bob, not only free of leprosy, but missing fingers restored as well. As Bob spoke about Jesus, the light from the campfire danced in his eyes like the stars in the heavens above. His words jumped with hope, and so did Leah's heart. If Jesus healed Bob, he could heal her, couldn't he?

Like the pegs of a poorly made stool, Leah's legs wobbled. She gritted her teeth, willing strength into her limbs, but no strength came. Staggering sideways, Leah collapsed into a heap at the side of the roadway.

Sarah rushed back to her and helped Leah upright. "Here, take some water."

Leah eagerly drank from the water skin propped against her sister's chest.

"Are you ready to give up this foolishness?"

"No," Leah said. "I have to get to him. Just a little rest. That's all I need."

"You need more than a little rest. You need food and sleep. We have to find shelter and prepare for the night."

Leah shook her head. "No. I'm going to get to Jesus. I'm sick of being an outcast."

"Better a live outcast than a dead woman!"

Leah pulled herself to a sitting position and turned to Sarah. "No, Sarah, better dead than an outcast. Do you have any idea what it's like to never be allowed to touch anyone? Never to feel another person's hand in yours? I am dead, Sarah. My heart just hasn't stopped yet."

Sarah reached forward and touched her cheek. "There, feel my hand. I don't care if you make me unclean. I'll come to your home as often as I can, I'll hold your hand for as long as you want. Just give up this silly adventure."

Leah took Sarah's hand in hers. "And what will happen when you go home? Will you touch Father? Will you let him be unclean without him knowing it?"

Sarah looked away.

Leah touched Sarah's cheek and turned her sister to face her.

"That's right, Sarah. You can't lie to Father. You'll tell him, and he'll either tell you not to see me or he'll cast you from the house too. It's enough this curse rests on me without you having to suffer too. The only way out of this prison is death or Jesus. Now, help me up."

Sarah stood and reached down to Leah. Leah struggled to her feet, walked a few paces, and then felt her legs give way beneath her.

"No!" Leah screamed. "This isn't fair."

Sarah crouched beside her. "Leah, your body can't take any more. This is a hard walk for anyone, never mind someone who always bleeds. Eat some food; drink some water. Give yourself a chance to recover."

Leah nodded her head.

Sarah held out her hand. "Let's try to get off the road."

Leah let her sister help her to her feet, and by leaning against Sarah, managed to get off the road before collapsing again.

Sarah rummaged through Leah's bag and dug out the dried dates and nuts Leah had packed and handed them to her.

"Thank you," Leah said. "You should have some too."

"I'm fine," Sarah said. "You just eat and get some strength. I'm obviously not going to be able to talk you out of this, so at least try to give yourself a fighting chance."

Leah chewed the food, but the sun creeping across the sky ate up the daylight. If she didn't get going soon it would be dark, and the chances of finding Jesus would be slim. She finished the food, drank some more water, and then moved to get up.

Sarah put her hand on Leah's shoulder. "No you don't. You need more rest."

"Look at the sun."

"If the sun goes down, we'll just sleep here, then start again tomorrow."

Leah settled back down, but despair chewed away at her soul. What if Jesus moved on? The leper said he moved around a lot, never staying at one place for long. She wanted to beat her legs, punish them for failing to get her where she needed to go—but what good would that do?

Leah forced herself to remain still while the sun mocked her. Nothing could stop its march across the sky. It consumed time like a wolf devouring a helpless lamb. Her eyelids drooped. Leah tried to will them open, but fatigue won the battle.

Leah's eyes fluttered open. "What did you say?"

"I said I wonder what all the commotion is."

Fully awake, Leah heard voices in the distance. A boy of twelve rounded the corner, half running, half skipping.

"What's happening?" Sarah called to the boy.

"Jesus is coming. He's going to perform a miracle, and I want to get there first so I can get a good place to watch."

Leah struggled to her feet. "Jesus is coming?"

The boy nodded his head as he passed by.

Sarah took her arm, and with her sister's help, Leah hobbled to the road just as the crowd came in sight. The leper described him as an ordinary-looking man, but Leah had no problem figuring out which of the group was Jesus. Everyone's attention was focused on one man.

Leah broke free from her sister. Hope overwhelmed despair, and strength flowed into her limbs. She let the crowd pass and then moved up behind him. She couldn't touch him or she'd make him unclean. But surely it would be all right to touch his clothes. If she touched his clothes, surely that's all she'd need to be healed.

Leah was within an arms' reach of Jesus. He didn't turn; he just kept on walking and talking to those around him. Her hand shook uncontrollably as she reached forward. She touched his garment.

It felt like a summer rain descended upon her. Warm water ran down from her head to her feet. Cramps melted away; the flow had stopped.

Jesus stopped. Leah froze. He knew what she'd done. What would he do to her?

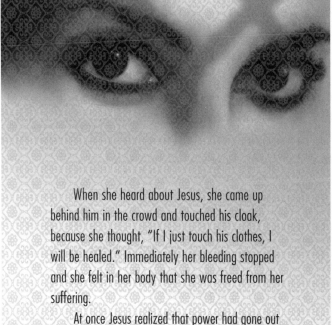

When she heard about Jesus, she came up behind him in the crowd and touched his cloak, because she thought, "If I just touch his clothes, I will be healed." Immediately her bleeding stopped and she felt in her body that she was freed from her suffering.

At once Jesus realized that power had gone out from him. He turned around in the crowd and asked, "Who touched my clothes?"

"You see the people crowding against you," his disciples answered, "and yet you can ask, 'Who touched me?'"

But Jesus kept looking around to see who had done it. Then the woman, knowing what had happened to her, came and fell at his feet and, trembling with fear, told him the whole truth. He said to her, "Daughter, your faith has healed you. Go in peace and be freed from your suffering." (Mark 5:27–34 NIV)

Wow! I don't think any of us can even begin to imagine how this woman felt at that moment of healing. Twelve years of being an outcast, of suffering in pain, and one touch and it's all gone.

You just gotta love Jesus and his reaction to this unclean, outcast woman. Christianity has a bit of a bad rap for being a religion that puts women down. Really? If that were the case, when the woman went to touch Jesus, here's what he would've said:

> What do you think you are trying to do? Don't touch me. I don't want to be unclean. Besides, do you think I've got time to deal with a woman's silly complaint? Eve messed up in the garden of Eden; you'll just have to live with it. There are lepers out there who need to be healed, blind who need to see, deaf to hear, dumb to speak. Right now, I'm on the way to raise a girl from the dead. Get away, woman. I don't have time for such a trivial problem as yours.

That's not what happened, was it? A uniquely female complaint wasn't too much trouble for the Son of God to stop for a moment and heal. What a message that must've sent to the crowd! He even made sure everyone in the crowd knew what type of illness he'd healed, because "then the woman … told him the whole truth."

News flash from Jesus to men everywhere: "I care about women's unique problems, and you should too."

And then there's her faith. Jesus said, "Your faith

has healed you." Where in the world did this woman get that kind of faith?

You know, there's an old proverb: "Fool me once, shame on you; fool me twice, shame on me." It's easy to fool someone the first time because we tend to trust people. Once someone has betrayed our trust, we shouldn't be fooled by them again. If we are, it's our own fault.

I think it's safe to say that after all she'd been through, Leah had every reason to crawl into a hole and wait for death. She trusted each physician, and each one made her worse. But something happened to kindle that little spark of faith in her. The Scriptures don't say what that was, but in keeping with my theory that she lived with the lepers, look back at Mark 1:40–45:

> Now a leper came to Him, imploring Him, kneeling down to Him and saying to Him, "If You are willing, You can make me clean."
>
> Then Jesus, moved with compassion, stretched out His hand and touched him, and said to him, "I am willing; be cleansed." As soon as He had spoken, immediately the leprosy left him, and he was cleansed. And He strictly warned him and sent him away at once, and said to him, "See that you say nothing to anyone; but go your way, show yourself to the priest, and offer for your cleansing those things which Moses commanded, as a testimony to them."
>
> However, he went out and began to proclaim it freely, and to spread the matter, so that Jesus could no longer openly enter the

city, but was outside in deserted places; and
they came to Him from every direction.

Yep, this former leper just couldn't keep his mouth
shut. So full of joy, he just had to share it with everyone who would listen—and I believe Leah was one of
those people who heard his testimony.

That must've been the spark that kindled the flame of
faith in Leah's heart. The desperation of her condition would
blow on that flame to make it grow. Faced with the evidence
of a leper now clean, Leah would just have to find Jesus.

She probably heard some of the other stories too:
demons getting their eviction papers, pigs doing belly
flops off a cliff into the sea. The buzz around Jesus
must've been incredible. To a woman as desperate as
Leah, that buzz would have dragged her to him like a
marathon runner to Gatorade.

And this is another thing I love about Jesus. He
didn't just wander on to the scene and proclaim in a
loud voice, "Hey, everyone, Son of God here, time to
repent, believe in me, and receive eternal life." No, he
gave plenty of evidence to back up his claims: miracles,
signs, and wonders to cultivate the seed of faith that is
in the heart of those who seek God.

He cultivated that seed in Leah, and through that
faith she finally found healing for her body. But more
than that, she found healing for her soul.

But what about us? Do we have many bona fide
miracles these days? What signs and wonders does
God provide to kindle our faith?

> Jesus said to him, "Thomas, because you
> have seen Me, you have believed. Blessed
> are those who have not seen and yet have
> believed. (John 20:29)

We have the written record of the events that surrounded Jesus' ministry on earth—a written record more
reliable than many historical documents the modern
world accepts as fact. We have the testimony of the original witnesses as to what happened. Enough yet?

We have a church history of people dying for believing in Jesus Christ as God's son. Refer to *Foxe's Book of
Martyrs* to see how many of the apostles died for
Christianity. Most of them suffered a violent death. Who
in their right mind suffers violent deaths for a lie? Sure,
one or two could have been crazy, but all of them?

We live on a planet so complex that the chances of
it coming into being in its present form by evolution-
ary means or cosmic accident are similar to the
chances of throwing a bomb in a junkyard and having
a Boeing 747 appear.

But the greatest witness of Jesus is a criminal biker
who becomes a preacher, a drug addict who cleans up
and supports his family, a businessman who finds true
value not in money but in a relationship with God, or a
woman of the night who becomes a woman of the light.

There are plenty of miracles; we just need to open
our eyes to see them. Every person whose life has
somehow been touched, changed, or healed by an
encounter with Jesus is a whole collection of miracles

all in one place. It doesn't take faith to experience a miracle, necessarily, but it does take faith to help us see the miracles that already surround us.

Probably the most life-changing miracle in my life was during the recession of 1980, when I was blessed enough to have a full-time job pumping gas. Not too glorious, but it kept my family fed and a roof over our heads. Unfortunately, the amount of walking the job required aggravated a birth defect in my left knee to the point I couldn't work anymore.

So I lost that job and ended up on unemployment-insurance sick benefits while I waited for surgery. In Canada, everyone gets medical care—sometimes it's just a matter of when.

I really didn't like sitting around, so I decided to invoke my rights under James 5:14:

> Is anyone among you sick? Let him call for
> the elders of the church, and let them pray
> over him, anointing him with oil in the name
> of the Lord.

And that's exactly what I did. The elders and the pastor gathered around me, poured oil on my head, and asked the Lord to heal my knee.

And wouldn't you know it—he didn't.

Yeah, that's right, my knee still hurt. I still needed surgery. I went through the usual doubts about whether or not God really meant his promises. Then I moved from there to maybe I just didn't have enough faith to get the job done. After all, it was faith that healed the woman with the issue of the blood.

Or maybe God just preferred to use the doctors to perform his miracle. Yeah, I decided, that's the answer. The doctors will be his instrument.

The day finally came. They operated on my knee—and you know what? That knee still hurts to this day—just not as much.

So, with no miracle in hand, my life went on. Bored with no work, I started attending a men's morning prayer meeting at my church. After study of the Scripture and general prayer, these guys would gather around those who didn't have a job and pray that God would bless them with work. Remember, there was a recession on, so plenty of guys were in the same boat as me.

Initially I hung back and didn't participate, preferring to see how these other guys did. Wouldn't you know it? They were getting jobs. So, one morning I stepped into the circle and had these men pray for me.

Armed with the assurance God would now get me a job, I went to the local unemployment office to check the job board. There was absolutely nothing I was suitable for. Even though I had had the surgery, my knee was far from 100 percent.

I started down the stairway of the building and ran into the government worker who handled my case. I told her of my frustration at not being able to find work, especially now with this knee problem. She mentioned something about the Labor Department having a program for disabled people and gave me a number to call.

Once home, I called the number and talked to a fellow in charge of retraining programs, and he made it pretty clear there probably wasn't much he could do for me—but he scheduled a home visit anyway.

The day of the visit, I opened the door and this stern man in his early fifties stood there. He looked past me up the stairs to my two-year-old daughter standing behind the child-safety gate. Sarah stood there grinning, with her soother hanging half out of her mouth. The man cracked a smile.

He came upstairs, looked around, said hi to my wife, then asked a few questions about my injury. I made it clear I wasn't really that disabled and in time, I'd be able to run and do any kind of work.

He looked straight at me and said, "Can you pump gas?"

"No."

"Then you're disabled."

I raised an eyebrow. "Are you sure?"

He smiled. "Disabled is what I say it is, and I say you're disabled. Go to the college; find a program you want to take. My department will pay all your tuition, books, and a living allowance for the next two years."

My wife and I couldn't believe our ears. I went to the college, enrolled in the accounting program, and that led to my becoming a Certified General Accountant. (That's similar to being a CPA in the United States.)

God clearly gave us favor in the eyes of this government official. And God did keep his promise of James 5:14, because James 5:15 says,

And the prayer of faith will save the sick,
and the Lord will raise him up. And if he has
committed sins, he will be forgiven.

God did save me, and he did raise me up. That
education has enabled me to enjoy a decent standard
of living. He could've healed my knee, and I would
have gone back to pumping gas. He could've given me
a job that day, and I'd probably still be struggling to
make ends meet. God clearly kept his promise and
performed a miracle in my life; I just didn't know it
until he was finished.

There have been miracles in your life too. You just
have to open your eyes to see them. Remember, Jesus
performed many miracles, and yet many didn't believe.
They didn't want to see, so they were blind.

But you want to see, so open your eyes. Let the
miracles of everyday life that surround you nurture
that seed of faith within you—the faith that God is on
his throne, that he cares deeply for you, and no matter
what happens, he's got a plan, and you're part of it.

Leah's faith brought her healing and hope at the
hands of the Son of God. Let her faith now be the cat-
alyst that leads you to those heart-healing hands as
well.

3

BAD DAY TO BE A DEMON

(Delivered)

Mary Magdalene rocked back and forth and moaned near the side of the road. Inside her head, voices argued with each other. One wanted her to bash her head against a rock; another wanted her to tear at her skin. Her eyes darted like a frightened fox looking for a way of escape. She'd tried running more times than she could remember; but the voices stayed with her.

She saw a group of travelers coming. Maybe they could help. Mary jumped to her feet and rushed at the men before the voices could react. She opened her mouth to plead for help, but one of the voices took over. Instead, she hurled insults and foul words at the men.

The men stopped and shrank back from her. Next thing Mary knew, she was pulling at her hair and lunging at them. Try as she might, she couldn't will her feet to turn the other way. Next, she was spitting at them along with the insults.

A lanky fellow stepped forward and yelled at her while motioning with his hands. Mary felt like she was watching from somewhere else while she jumped at him and scratched his face. Pain exploded in her shoulder as the man punched her. Mary wanted to run; the voices wanted to fight. She spat and kicked at him.

The man tried to catch her flailing fists, but Mary had strength that wasn't her own. She caught him in the nose with her fist and blood flowed freely over his mouth. He dropped back, and Mary turned her rage—no, it turned its rage—on the other three.

She rushed toward the nearest one, and her head snapped back when his fist caught her on the cheek. Mary howled in pain, but the voices pushed her on. She punched; he punched back. His fist caught her underneath the chin, and Mary's legs lost their strength. Mercifully, she collapsed to the ground and darkness silenced the voices.

Mary's eyes fluttered open. The voices were silent. Through blurred vision, she saw the road a few feet away. At least these men had the decency to drag her off the road and leave her be. Other times Mary hadn't been so fortunate.

She struggled to a sitting position and her stomach roiled with nausea. Mary took a few long, deep breaths and waited for the world to settle down before attempting to stand. She touched her puffy lips and rolled her tongue around her mouth, gingerly touching the cuts inside her mouth. There'd been worse incidents.

Mary got to her feet and wobbled to the road. With every step, she regained some clarity and managed to pick up the pace in spite of the throbbing in her head. The sun would soon set, and she didn't want to be on the road at dark. It wasn't a safe place even for a crazy woman.

The voices mumbled a bit in the background but seemed to be willing to let her have her own thoughts, go her own direction—for now. They were always more subdued after she'd been beaten. Maybe that's why pounding her head against the ground seemed to help silence them.

As twilight started to settle, Mary took a path off the road to where she and others like her spent their nights. They lived in the caves away from everyone. Not even the lepers would permit these women to live near them.

The smell of roasted flesh wafted to her nose, and Mary's stomach jumped to a rumble. When had she last eaten? She couldn't remember.

Darkness enveloped the path, but Mary could see a fire through the brush. She felt her way to the promised warmth and safety of the flames—not to mention the food. Hopefully, whoever brought it would share.

Mary broke free from the brush and picked up the pace to cover the short distance between the brush and the caves. She saw a group of women huddled around the fire tearing into chunks of meat. Now she ran, hoping to get there before it was all gone.

No one looked at her as Mary forced her way into the circle. The half-roasted carcass of some animal lay beside the fire. Mary didn't dare try to figure out what it might have been. She just tore into its flesh like the others and grunted in satisfaction when the meat hit her empty stomach.

Mary felt strength returning to her weary body as her stomach did its job. She also heard the voices start to talk amongst themselves. That's why they'd been so silent. So she could eat. She was no use to them hungry.

Mary looked around the fire at the eyes of the other women. They were changing too. They were hearing voices. She backed away from the fire while she still had some control over her own body. The other women started to argue amongst themselves. A voice urged her to go back, to tell these women what she really thought of them.

Mary dropped to her knees and howled in anguish. She wanted to run away, but they wouldn't let her feet take her in any direction but back to the quarreling women. The voices began to gang up on her now. They wouldn't stop until she went back and joined in the melee they were planning.

She groaned as she tried to prevent her legs from moving back to the fire. Mary had already endured one beating today. Her mouth started to move and uttered insulting words at the other women. The fight was on.

Mary gave as good as she got. Fists flew, hair was pulled, and she ended up on the ground. It was morning when Mary regained consciousness.

She slowly sat up and gently touched her split lips. Mary had trouble seeing out of her left eye, and one touch confirmed it had swelled almost completely shut. A deep breath was cut short by sharp pain in her ribs. Mary feared she wouldn't survive many more nights like this.

The other women started to stir. From her good eye, Mary could see they hadn't faired too well either. They all looked at her and started to mumble. Coldness crept up Mary's spine. They were still hearing the voices, and the voices were telling them to hurt her, maybe even kill her.

Mary scrambled to her feet and started to the bushes. Curses followed her and she could hear the women in pursuit. She broke into the brush, pushing branches aside as she fled toward the road. Maybe there she could find someone to help her.

A voice in her head laughed. It said there would be no help for her. Why wouldn't the voices help her? Didn't they need her to live?

Mary's foot caught on a root and she tumbled to the ground. She ignored the flames of pain in her ribs and used a small tree to pull herself to her feet. Feet pummeling the ground drew closer. Mary took what breath she could and started to run again.

She ran, ignoring small branches whipping at her face and arms, cutting into her flesh. She ran until she neared the road — then the voices screamed for her to stop, to go no farther.

The other women caught up to her; they all staggered to a stop. Something was wrong; they weren't attacking her.

The voices were becoming quiet; Mary sensed something; they were afraid of something, something on the road.

With every shred of her own will she had left, Mary forced her feet one step ahead of the other. Suddenly a flash of a fond memory broke past the voices. She remembered little girls hanging on to her feet while she pulled them along. Who were those children? Sisters? Mary couldn't remember, but her feet moved easier now, like they only had to drag small children along.

She stepped out from the bushes and shielded her eyes from the morning sun. A man's voice drifted on the cool air. The demons chorused in fear. They grabbed at her mouth and forced her jaws shut. They weren't afraid; they were terrified of this voice.

But Mary wasn't afraid of the voice. It reminded her of cool water running down a parched throat. It reminded her of a warm bed on a cold night. It reminded her of the safety of her father's arms. Mary started toward the voice, ignoring the threats of death and violence the voices uttered.

They released her mouth and started working on her feet again. Instead of dragging two small children, Mary felt like she was dragging heavy bags of grain. She labored with every step and made slow, painful progress toward the voice. She looked behind her and saw the other women having similar battles of their own to get to this voice, to the voice that made the other voices tremble.

Mary called words of encouragement to the women, then gritted her teeth and bore on. She reached the crest of a rise in the road and saw a group of men seated in a semicircle around a fire, listening to the one with the voice.

Her heart pounded with hope, and the voices howled in despair. Suddenly they released her feet. Mary ran to the man with the voice; she ran in spite of the throbbing pain in her head; she ran in spite of the flames burning in her ribs; she ran in spite of the horrible things the voices threatened if she didn't stop.

The men all turned to look at her and the women who followed her. They shrank away—all except the man with the voice. Mary Magdalene collapsed before him and wept. Everything went quiet.

Mary struggled to her feet. The man was speaking, but she couldn't hear anything. The voices were filling her ears so she couldn't hear him.

Mary howled in despair. All she wanted to do was hear again that voice that felt like a soothing balm on blistered skin. Mary's eyes met the man's eyes, and even though she couldn't hear her own words, she begged him to help her.

He stood. His face hardened. His eyes looked directly into hers, and he spoke only a few words that Mary never heard. What she did hear was an unearthly screech from the voices as they screamed in agony. They exploded from her body, and Mary could hear their cries of anguish as they faded away.

Mary's knees buckled, and she stumbled face forward to the ground. Complete and utter exhaustion overtook her, and for the first time in as long as she could remember, Mary fell asleep knowing she was completely safe.

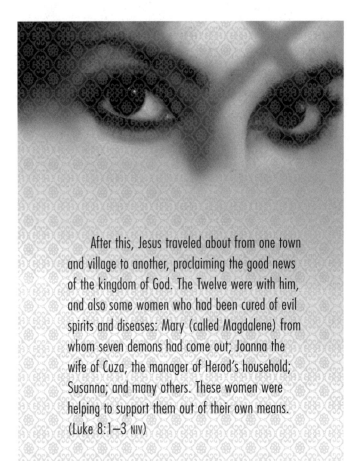

After this, Jesus traveled about from one town and village to another, proclaiming the good news of the kingdom of God. The Twelve were with him, and also some women who had been cured of evil spirits and diseases: Mary (called Magdalene) from whom seven demons had come out; Joanna the wife of Cuza, the manager of Herod's household; Susanna; and many others. These women were helping to support them out of their own means. (Luke 8:1–3 NIV)

The Scriptures don't really tell us anything about how Mary Magdalene came to be demon possessed or demon dispossessed. What we do know is that when she met Jesus, he delivered her from a life of torturous sorrow.

In these modern times, being delivered really doesn't have much going for it. Pizza is delivered, newspapers are delivered, babies are delivered—but people aren't delivered. In Mary Magdalene's time, being delivered meant being set free from the bondage of Satan. It was a big deal.

When Jesus walked the earth, being delivered was huge news. Once set free you'd probably jump up and down in excitement, then run home to tell the family who kicked you out that it was okay for you to come home. Being delivered was front-page news way back when.

Today, in the Western world, most people don't believe demon possession is a problem anymore. Of course, we probably also have the most addictions in history. We have drug addiction, alcohol addiction, sex addiction, food addiction, money addiction, and whatever-else-you-can-think-of addiction.

And the great news is that Jesus can deliver us from all these addictions. But what Jesus delivered me from is greater than being set free from every addiction out there—he delivered me from a pointless life.

A pointless life?

Until I met Jesus Christ, I led a pointless life. I was in my early twenties and working as a pipe fitter's apprentice on heavy-construction projects. We built some incredible stuff like pulp mills, newsprint machines, and even the Revelstoke Dam, which provides power to western North America. All these projects were marvelous achievements, but they were pointless when compared to knowing Jesus Christ.

At that time, I lived in construction camps with hundreds of other men. My life was a prescription in futility: wake up, eat, go to work, eat, go drinking, go to bed—repeat until dead.

At first I really enjoyed this life. The food they served in construction camps was incredible. They served T-bone steak at least twice a weak, and their dessert table would put most bakeries to shame—going hungry just wasn't an option.

But believe it or not, week in and week out of gourmet food became routine. Suddenly T-bone steak went from being a treat to just another meal. Western omelets with thick buttered toast were no more interesting than a bowl of cereal. I know this sounds hard to believe, but one can get sick of fantastic food.

As a young man, I found the nights of drinking thrilling at first. I'd go to the nightclub with my newfound construction friends and drink to get drunk. With the alcohol coursing my veins, I'd have the courage to move on to the next project—chasing women.

It took me awhile to realize my complete and utter failure in chasing women might have had something to do with being drunk. It seems women aren't particularly impressed by young men who are so drunk they have trouble keeping their balance and keeping their mouths from saying stupid things.

I spent about a year and half on that treadmill of futility. It took more of everything to generate any kind of pleasure. While I was laughing on the outside, I was empty on the inside. I was living a pointless life that brought no joy.

A single prayer knocked me off that path of meaninglessness. A single prayer set the course that would lead to my deliverance from an existence where I was really just a shell occupying space in this world.

I had a former girlfriend I'd previously lived with for a couple of years. She'd been on her own journey of futility. Like me, she'd reached a point where life just seemed to have no purpose. Her journey led her to people and books that talked about Jesus Christ. She read, she learned, and then she said a simple prayer that changed both our lives. She said, "Jesus, if you bring Andy back, I'll follow you."

Only once during my journey can I remember encountering the gospel. One of my construction buddies was saved and came back and told us all about it. On the outside we mocked him and predicted he'd be back to carousing with us in no time. Inside, I envied him. I instinctively knew he'd found something good.

Also, in our pursuit of feminine company we would come across "religious" girls. Here's something you need to know if you're one of those girls. Those were the girls we respected. The girls who said no were the ones who really got our interest. Sure, on the outside we said things like, "Call me if you ever change your mind." On the inside, we thought, *Wow, maybe I should clean up my act if getting a girl like her is the result.*

Take it from an ex-reprobate construction worker: The worst that can happen when you say no is the guy will walk away and never call you again. If you say yes, he'll probably hang around for a while, then take off when he's bored—and he'll never call you again. There's no downside to no, plenty of downside to yes.

The first thing that happened after my former girlfriend prayed is that I had an accident. I strained the muscles in my shoulder pulling up a section of scaffolding. The strain was bad enough that the doctor told me to take a week off work. *Great,* I thought. I might as well go home.

So I hopped into my car and drove back to Langley, British Columbia, to my parents' house. When I got home, my older brother, also a construction worker, was there visiting. He was occupying my bedroom. I found this highly offensive, as I sent money home every month to keep that bedroom available for me. (My mother remembers this differently, just in case you ever talk to her.)

I crashed emotionally at that point. All that eating, drinking, and carousing had brought no lasting joy. And now I didn't even have my own bedroom. I could remember only one time when I was happy—when I was with my girlfriend.

To be clear, I never stopped loving her. While we were apart, a day didn't pass that I didn't think of her. Oh, I might as well be honest. Five waking minutes didn't pass without my thinking of her.

Our breakup was just one big mess of confusion and misunderstanding. What prevented me from calling was that I was under the impression she had found someone else.

But in that trench of despair, I phoned her. Even if she had another boyfriend, at least I could hear her voice. The conversation went something like this:

"Hi," I said.

"Hi," she said.

"So what are you up to?"

"Not much. Just living in a cabin on some friend's property. It's really pretty. It's in the forest and a stream runs right underneath it."

"Wow, that sounds great. Uh, so, uh, are you seeing anyone?"

Silence on her end. My heart pounded somewhere up in my throat.

"No. Are you?"

I didn't think my heart could pound harder, but it did. "No," I answered. "Uh, any chance you might want to visit?"

"Yes."

That "yes" might as well have been a full-blown orchestra playing the "Hallelujah" chorus from Handel's *Messiah*. I must have sent some sort of land-speed record from Langley to Revelstoke.

My girlfriend said a simple prayer that brought me back to her. But more important, I now was being exposed to the same people and books—the ones that talked about Jesus. I'm almost embarrassed to admit this, but most of those "books" were really Christian comic books. I found Jesus Christ through Christian comic books.

I would read these comic books voraciously, and they all had a similar theme: Someone was leading a pointless life until they met Jesus. I could identify with the stories. The characters' lives were the same as my life. Even though I was back with my girlfriend, I still knew there was a big, empty hole in my soul.

So, in a little cabin above a stream in a forest, I asked Jesus Christ to deliver me from my pointless life—and he did.

As for my girlfriend? By the time this book is in print, we will have celebrated our twenty-fifth wedding anniversary.

So what changed after that?

Well, life was still a routine. I still ate, went to work, came home, spent time with my girlfriend, then repeated. Even today, I sleep, I wake up, I go to work, I come home, I do something, I go to bed, and then I do it all over again. Sounds pretty pointless, doesn't it?

Maybe.

Imagine you're in Washington, DC, in a line at Starbucks. You strike up a conversation with a middle-aged woman in front of you. It goes something like this:

"Is it always busy like this?" you say.

"Just in the morning," the woman answers. "During the day it's not too bad. You're not from around here, are you?"

"Is it that obvious?"

"It's the accent," she says. "Louisiana?"

"Yeah."

"On vacation?"

You nod your head. "I've always wanted to see the nation's capital. I guess you work around here?"

She nods.

"What do you do?"

She smiles faintly. "I'm just one of the many secretaries in Washington."

You smile back. "Where do you work?"

She looks past you to the door. You glance behind you and there's a humorless man in a dark suit with dark glasses standing there. Your eyebrows jump up. "You work at the White House?"

She nods.

"Whose secretary are you?"

"I work for the president," she whispers. "Even though they have the same coffee back at the office, he says it doesn't taste the same."

One minute this woman was just a secretary, but now she's the president's secretary. She has instantaneous status and importance, even though the work she performs is the same as the work performed by hundreds of thousands of secretaries. Her work is important not because of what she does but who she does it for.

So the truth is any kind of life lived for Jesus is a life worth living because you're living for him. Maybe you're a stay-at-home mom without a "real" job. Now you have one. Your job is to raise those kids for God. You've gone from being a soccer mom to tutor of the King of Heaven's children.

Maybe you're a single mom. You've got two real jobs. You've got the job of raising kids on your own and perhaps a mundane job to feed them. Well, now you're raising Jesus' kids, and that mundane job is a means to support his children.

Maybe you're a highly regarded professional. Before Jesus, your profession really only served to make you financially comfortable until you gasp your last breath. And when you gasp that last breath, I doubt you'll be comforting yourself with your professional achievements.

Now your profession is a tool that Jesus can use to spread his gospel throughout the world. You can reach people others can't just because of your status in society.

The wonderful thing is Jesus delivers us from a great, big, fat lie of the world we live in: that what we do is what matters. Jesus says who you do it for is what matters. If you accept him into your heart and live for him, it doesn't matter what you do. You did it for him, and it now matters.

4

OFF THE TRACKS

(Slammed)

Issachar wandered about the outer court of the temple, fighting with his conscience. They were good women; they'd been kind to him. This would be a betrayal. No, he wasn't betraying them; he was exposing that blasphemer. Yes, he was doing his duty to God.

The middle-aged man took a deep breath and ambled over to a couple of temple guards. The one on the left boasted a thick black beard and barrel chest, while his partner was tall and muscular. Both looked down at him with contempt.

"Yes?" Barrel Chest said.

Issachar cleared his throat. "Is it true that ... um ... there is a reward for information about Jesus?"

Barrel Chest's eyes narrowed. "And how would you have information about Jesus that would interest us?"

"I've seen him."

Both guards let loose deep belly laughs. Issachar looked about nervously but no one seemed to pay special attention. "Why do you laugh?"

"Thousands have seen Jesus," Barrel Chest said.

"But I've seen him break our traditions."

"Who hasn't?"

Muscles stepped closer to Issachar. "Where have you seen him?"

Issachar chewed on his lip and looked down at the ground.

"Answer."

"In Bethany."

"Where in Bethany?"

"The home of Martha."

Barrel Chest looked at Muscles. "The name is familiar. I think it's on the list."

"Maybe you should ask," Muscles said.

Barrel Chest nodded and left the outer court.

"You stay here," Muscles said.

Issachar nodded.

A short time passed as an eternity before Barrel Chest came back.

"Follow me," he grunted.

Issachar followed Barrel Chest to a room close beside the temple. Barrel Chest opened the door and motioned for him to go in.

Issachar stepped into the room and dropped to his knees. Before him stood the high priest flanked by two members of the Sanhedrin. Issachar kept his face to the ground.

"Stand," the high priest commanded.

Issachar scrambled to his feet but kept his head lowered. Barrel Chest stood close behind him.

"What is your name?"

"Issachar."

"And I'm told you are a servant of Martha of Bethany?"

"Yes."

"And you have information about Jesus of Nazareth?

Issachar nodded.

The high priest moved to a seat and sat down. The two Sanhedrin members proceeded to stand at either side. The high priest motioned with his hand. "Tell me what you know."

"Martha received word Jesus was coming. She became frantic and started ordering me to set up the banquet hall. After that, she disappeared into the kitchen to prepare the food. Her sister, Mary, arrived a few minutes later and went into the kitchen to help Martha.

"It didn't take me too long to get the places arranged, but the kitchen preparations weren't going as well. I ..."

The high priest held up his hand. "I've no interest in food preparations. Tell me about Jesus and what he did that was important enough for you to come to me."

"Well, it's not so much what he did, but what he didn't do."

The high priest looked past him at Barrel Chest. "I hope my time isn't about to be wasted."

Barrel Chest jabbed him in the back.

"Oh, no, my lord," Issachar said.

The high priest's eyes bore into Issachar's. "Then get to the point."

"Jesus and his disciples arrived and took their places. Mary entered the room and stopped dead in her tracks. She put down the food she was carrying and immediately went over to where Jesus was and sat at his feet."

The high priest stiffened. "How do you mean—sat at his feet?"

"Like she was one of his disciples."

The two members of the Sanhedrin clucked and shook their heads; the high priest stroked his beard. "What happened next?"

"Martha entered with more food and started serving. She kept looking over at Mary, who ignored her and sat listening to Jesus. Finally Martha asked Jesus to tell her sister to get up and help."

"And what did Jesus do?"

"Nothing."

The high priest lifted his eyebrows. "Nothing?"

"In fact, he rebuked Martha."

"He what?"

"He told her to quit worrying and that Mary was doing the right thing."

One of the members of the Sanhedrin turned to the high priest. "He treats a woman as a disciple, tells her to forsake her duty. Can you imagine what would happen if all women acted so? Our traditions would crumble; our society would be lost. Something must be done."

"Yes," the high priest said. "Something will be done."

He looked at Issachar. "If this Jesus returns to your master's home, you are to watch him and to report to us what he does. Understood?"

Issachar nodded his head.

"You may go."

He started to back out of the room then stopped. "Um . . ."

"What?" the high priest said.

"There were rumors of a reward."

The high priest stroked his beard again. "Of course there is a reward. You have the reward of knowing you are serving your God. Is that not enough?"

Issachar nodded his head rapidly.

"Then go."

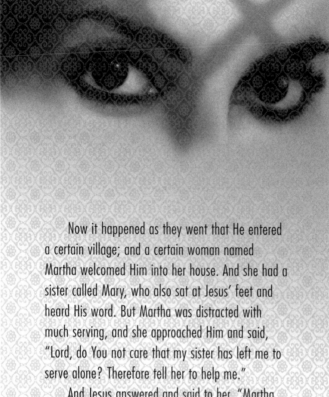

Now it happened as they went that He entered a certain village; and a certain woman named Martha welcomed Him into her house. And she had a sister called Mary, who also sat at Jesus' feet and heard His word. But Martha was distracted with much serving, and she approached Him and said, "Lord, do You not care that my sister has left me to serve alone? Therefore tell her to help me."

And Jesus answered and said to her, "Martha, Martha, you are worried and troubled about many things. But one thing is needed, and Mary has chosen that good part, which will not be taken away from her." (Luke 10:38–42)

I think Martha was one of those women who liked order. Things are supposed to be done a certain way and in a certain time. Jesus and his friends showed up, and Martha probably thought, *We have guests and we have to feed them.*

When Mary opted out of helping so she could listen to Jesus, that didn't fit in with Martha's way of doing things. Mary's behavior created disorder. Mary's behavior slammed Martha off the path of her ordered life.

I got slammed once. Heavy snowfall had rendered the road only slightly better than an ice rink. The driver in front of me was having trouble keeping control of his car. It was clear to me he'd never driven in snow before. When he lost traction he'd punch the accelerator and start to fishtail, which only made matters worse.

I was a teenager, I was late for work, and I was losing patience with this snow-traveler wannabe. My chance came when he spun out and careened to the other side of the road. I plowed on and passed him on the right. It was my bad luck he spun out again right back into my lane and slammed me.

Getting slammed hurts. My whole body rocked with the impact and I ended up disoriented. One second I'm on my way to work, the next, I'm trying to avoid the ditch.

During the time of Mary and Martha, women got slammed all the time. They had a defined role in their culture: cook, clean, and bear children—preferably sons. Step out of line and there was a whole culture ready to slam you.

When Jesus entered her home, I wonder if Mary paused before she sat at his feet. Did she look at all those men around him and wonder what they would do? Her heart probably tried to jump out of her chest to get to him, but like an out-of-control automobile, a whole culture stood ready to slam her.

But Mary probably took a deep breath and ignored the possible slamming. When Mary sat at Jesus' feet, she became a revolutionary because she assumed the posture of a disciple. This was an incredibly major no-no. It just wasn't done. I read a sermon by a Dr. Kim Hauenstein that said,

> *Only* males could serve as disciples to the great teachers of the day; only males could discuss with their teacher the meanings and nuances of the Torah and other religious writings.[1]

When Martha saw this happen, she must have been beside herself. I'm not so sure that her concern about Mary's not helping wasn't more about the consequences of Mary's thumbing her nose at their culture. It's possible her motivation for appealing to Jesus was to get him to set her sister straight about her cultural role before something bad happened.

But Jesus didn't do that, did he? Instead, he decided to slam the culture that treated women like property. He said, "Mary has chosen that good part, which will not be taken away from her." He made it clear right then that women are just as important to the kingdom of God as men. They are to learn about God just as men are, and, yes, they can ask questions.

This had serious ramifications for him. According to the code of the day, he should've rebuked Mary. He set a frightening precedent that would have the patriarchal culture of the day twisting in knots. Prophets had been killed for less. Jesus risked his life by encouraging Mary rather than rebuking her.

Dr. Hauenstein further comments,

> I remind you again that this is an issue that would get him into trouble. Jesus continually engages women in public conversation, which is against the social and religious code. Men were *not* to speak to women in public. Jesus did so, and on a regular basis. He turned that religious and social code upside down.

The culture that slammed women all the time would now be looking to slam Jesus, and as we all know, slam him it did.

Mary didn't let the culture slam her; Martha did. Martha was driving like I was driving. Instead of slowing down and seeing what was happening in front of her, she just put her head down and plowed on with the mundane tasks of life. And those tasks slammed her so that she missed the obvious.

God had come over for lunch.

Think of it for a moment. This is the guy who spoke the universe into existence. He actually understands the concepts of eternity, endless space, and how they get the caramel into the Caramilk bar. Mary sensed that; Martha didn't. Jesus was saying something important, and Mary dropped everything to hear it.

So what did Jesus expect Martha to do? Drop everything and join Mary? Yeah, he probably did.

Notice he says to her, "You are worried and troubled about many things." The cares of the world slammed Martha so hard she couldn't even recognize when her creator entered the room.

Maybe her thoughts were preoccupied with Lazarus. It's reasonable to assume that Lazarus was ill, considering he died not too long after this visit. Maybe she was trying to figure out how to pay the doctor bills. Or maybe it was something as superficial as worrying that her reputation for putting on a good spread was at stake.

As long as we inhabit this mortal body, we'll have something to be "worried and troubled about." Jesus isn't asking that we quit our jobs, quit paying our bills, and let our homes and families fall into disarray. But what he is asking is don't let those things slam us off the path of following him. He wants us to slow down and see them for what they really are.

If we don't, then we run the real risk that Jesus will walk into our homes and we'll treat our Savior no differently than we would a neighbor coming over for tea.

It's no secret that this world isn't our home. The apostle Paul writes,

> These all died in faith, not having received the promises, but having seen them afar off were assured of them, embraced *them* and confessed that they were strangers and pilgrims on the earth. (Heb. 11:13)

And yet we get carried away with this world. We let its cares and troubles become our cares and troubles. Why do most of us—myself included—live like Martha? Why do we let this very temporary existence slam us off the path of worshipping our creator?

As I write this chapter, it's day five of the hurricane Katrina disaster. I find the parallels between this tragedy and our own spiritual condition startling.

Imagine: One day you live in New Orleans, a world-famous city with all the modern comforts—clean water, electricity, and homes with roofs that don't leak. Want a coffee? There's a Starbucks just around the corner. Need something to eat? There's everything from McDonald's to the finest Cajun restaurants.

Next day, a hurricane slams the coastline with sheet after sheet of rain driven by ferocious winds. Waves crash against the levees; they break, and water floods the city streets. When it's all over, your home is gone, your city is gone, and suddenly you're a stranger in your own country, a refugee. Talk about getting slammed!

But wait a minute, you say. I'm a citizen of the United States. We're the most powerful country in the world—how can I be a refugee? You climb up onto a roof with other citizens waiting for help, but help isn't coming.

Someone comes up with the idea to arrange furniture and other debris to form the word *HELP* on the roof. Along with everyone else, you go into the building below, taking whatever will suit the task. After a day of hard work, you and your fellow survivors let your country know in letters easily visible from the air that you need HELP. And you each expect it because you're U.S. citizens.

Think of the hurricane as everyday life. Life relentlessly slams the levees of your spirit. The wind howls, the rain strafes the levees, driving the waves of everyday care against them. The levees look strong enough, but suddenly cracks form. Water dribbles through, then pours through, and finally the levees give way. Before you know it, you're scrambling for high ground just to avoid being swept away with the flood.

Now you find yourself sloshing through water up to your hips, wondering how you ended up in this mess. No home, no clean water, no food. Soon the storm clouds of complete and utter despair roll in. Wait a minute, you say. I'm a child of God. I have rights. Why am I wading in water mixed with sewage and things I don't even want to think about?

You feel just as abandoned as many of the people of the Gulf Coast felt. But you feel even more abandoned; because it isn't a government that's let you

down, it's God. You're in a swirling muck of polluted
water, and he's nowhere to be found.

Ever felt like this? I have. And when I take a
moment to be honest with myself, I realize I'm the one
who let the levees fall into disrepair. I'm the one who
let the cares of this world slam me from the mission of
living for Christ. When I look in the mirror I see
Martha, not Mary—and Mary chose the best part.

So we're wading through an above-ground sewer,
and life isn't all we'd hoped it would be. Where do we
go from here?

Let's follow the example of the people of New
Orleans. Let's get some furniture and junk and form
the word *HELP.* In other words, let's make talking to
God the first thing we do every single day. The nice
thing about God is we can abandon him as much as we
like, yet he sits waiting by the phone for our call. Don't
believe me? The Lord said,

> And Jesus came and spoke to them, saying,
> "All authority has been given to Me in
> heaven and on earth. Go therefore and
> make disciples of all the nations, baptizing
> them in the name of the Father and of the
> Son and of the Holy Spirit, teaching them to
> observe all things that I have commanded
> you; and lo, I am with you always, *even* to
> the end of the age." Amen. (Matt. 28:18–20)

Notice how long he's going to be with us—"even to

the end of the age." So just because we were slammed so hard we're not even sure what country we're a citizen of, that doesn't mean that God forgot who we are or where we are.

If you're having trouble with this idea of the creator of the universe taking so much abuse from his children, you're not a parent. My daughter turned out pretty good. She avoided a lot of the trouble teenagers get into and married a decent guy. I really have only one complaint. She and her husband tend to go against my advice on handling money and sometimes get in a bind.

So think about this situation. They went against my advice, did something inadvisable, and now they're in trouble. Do I refuse to help them? I'm well within my rights. They broke my law. They're on their own, right? Wrong.

Their car needed repairs. Both the brakes and snow tires were worn out, with winter fast approaching. There's no way I'm going to let my child travel in an unsafe car if it's in my means to do something about it. I don't care how silly she's been with her money. That's right; I lent them the money for the repairs. I hope to get it back someday, but if I don't, well, it's only money and I can always make more. I can't make another daughter exactly like the one I have.

We do silly things all the time and yet God's love never wavers. The fact is that most of us *think* we would give our lives for our children, but we know God has already given his Son for us.

In spite of the fact we've let our levees fall into

disrepair, our lives have been flooded with sin, and we feel alone, we're not. God just needs us to utter three little words. *God, help me.*

Try it.

Done it?

Good.

Now you're on the roof, and in the distance you can hear the whump-whump of helicopter blades cutting through the humid air.

Try this.

God, I want to come home.

Wow, that helicopter is overhead now. A crew chief is lowered to the roof. He straps you in, and before you know it, you're in the helicopter and being ferried away from the mess and destruction below. It isn't long before you're enjoying all the comforts you used to have. It isn't long before you're safe and secure.

But remember, God doesn't leave us; we leave God. It's crucial we talk to him every morning, even if just for a few moments. It's crucial we read his Word every morning so we're reminded we don't live in this world but the one to come. Then, if Jesus ever comes over for lunch, you'll be slamming down the serving spoon and rushing over to see what he's got to say.

5

THE WOMAN AT THE WELL

(Thirst)

    Abigail paused at the doorway and looked back at the bed. A hand hung out from underneath the bedclothes. The body it belonged to snored lustily under the covers. It was nearing the sixth hour and still he slept.

Abigail picked up the water jar by the door. When he woke up, he'd want water, and if it wasn't there, she'd hear about it all day long. Like it or not, she lived to serve him. Why did she keep making the same mistake over and over? They all seemed so nice at first.

Abigail took a deep breath at the door. Outside she would have to face the Whisperers and she would leave behind her the Whiner. What a life.

Once she stepped outside, Abigail kept her eyes to the ground lest she accidentally make eye contact with any of the women standing outside. They hated her; she hated them.

Was it her fault men found her attractive, that they enjoyed her company? If they concentrated more on keeping their men happy than on clucking at her when she walked past, maybe their husbands wouldn't have such wandering eyes. Who was Abigail kidding? At least they still had their original husbands.

After about fifteen minutes walking in the hot sun, Abigail was more than ready to draw some water and have a deep drink herself. She rounded the corner and stopped in her tracks. A man sat on the well, and from the looks of him, he was a Jew.

Just great. Now what should she do? She picked this time of day to avoid talking to anyone, and this Jew was sitting right on the well. What if some of the women happened by and saw her alone with the Jew? There would be no end to the conclusions they'd draw.

But Abigail couldn't go home. If she entered the house without water, the Whiner would just send her right back out again. She took a deep breath and strode to the well as if the Jew wasn't even there. She managed to steal a glance; he looked tired.

Abigail started to lower her jar into the well.

"Will you give me a drink?"

Abigail froze. The Jew just talked to her. Jews didn't talk to Samaritans. Was he trying to start some kind of trouble?

She stiffened, turned to face him, and said, with an edge to her voice, "You are a Jew and I am a Samaritan woman. How can you ask me for a drink?"

Instead of the usual sneer Jews gave Samaritans, a gentle smile spread across his face. "If you knew the gift of God and who it is that asks you for a drink, you would have asked him and he would have given you living water."

The generosity of God. What was he talking about? Maybe the hot sun was making him lightheaded.

"Sir," the woman said, "you have nothing to draw with and the well is deep. Where can you get this living water? Are you greater than our father Jacob, who gave us the well and drank from it himself, as did also his sons and his flocks and herds?"

The Jew shook his head. "Everyone who drinks this water will be thirsty again, but whoever drinks the water I give him will never thirst. Indeed, the water I give him will become in him a spring of water welling up to eternal life."

Any other man, any other time, and Abigail would be running and screaming. Living water, everlasting life, surely the sun had made him crazy. Abigail studied his face; this man wasn't crazy.

Suddenly she felt five years old again, sitting on her father's lap, held in his arms. That was the last time Abigail remembered feeling safe in her whole life. Her father died that night. A tear worked its way down her cheek. In this man's presence, she felt that way again.

"Sir, give me this water so that I won't get thirsty and have to keep coming here to draw water."

The smile faded from his face and his head tilted slightly. "Go, call your husband, and come back."

Abigail looked to the ground. She couldn't bring the Whiner. He'd accuse of her being with this godly man. He'd blab it to the whole town and maybe even throw her out. "I have no husband."

"You are right when you say you have no husband. The fact is, you have had five husbands, and the man you now have is not your husband. What you have just said is quite true."

Abigail's eyes widened. How could he know this about her? As a Jew, he couldn't have been hanging around her village and learned it from the gossips. Abigail took a deep breath and tried to steady her shaking knees. There was only one way this Jew could know.

"Sir," the woman said, "I can see that you are a prophet. Our fathers worshipped on this mountain, but you Jews claim that the place where we must worship is in Jerusalem."

He smiled at her like her father used to when she learned some small thing he tried to teach her.

"Believe me, woman, a time is coming when you will worship the Father neither on this mountain nor in Jerusalem. You Samaritans worship what you do not know; we worship what we do know, for salvation is from the Jews. Yet a time is coming and has now come when the true worshippers will worship the Father in spirit and truth, for they are the kind of worshippers the Father seeks. God is spirit, and his worshippers must worship in spirit and in truth."

Abigail held her breath. Did he mean what she thought he meant?

"I know that Messiah (called Christ) is coming. When he comes, he will explain everything to us."

He held her eyes for a moment. "I who speak to you am he."

Abigail went numb. This was all too incredible. The hope of centuries claimed he stood before her. Surely he was toying with her. No. He knew about the other men . . . and how could she explain how she felt in his presence? Part of her felt like a lost little girl whose father found her in the woods, and part of her felt afraid, very afraid. Abigail opened her mouth to speak, then heard voices nearing.

She looked to the right. Jewish men approached, and they

seemed none too pleased judging by the way they looked at her. She looked back at the man — Messiah? He made no sign that he even knew these men approached. Were they with him? What would they think? What would they do? Abigail trembled at the thought. Jews weren't known for their tolerance of her kind of woman.

Abigail dropped her water jar, spun, and fled back toward the town. Her heart pounded in her chest as her feet pounded the ground. Abigail flew past the women standing outside, their usual stares of contempt a blur. She drew up to the men of the village, her chest heaving as she tried to catch her breath.

They looked at her as if she were a crazy woman, and they'd think she was crazy once she told them about the ... Christ? Should she keep silent? No, this wasn't something she could ever keep silent about.

"Come, see a man who told me everything I ever did. Could this be the Christ?" (Dialogue of Jesus and the Samaritan woman are based on John 4:7–29 NIV.)

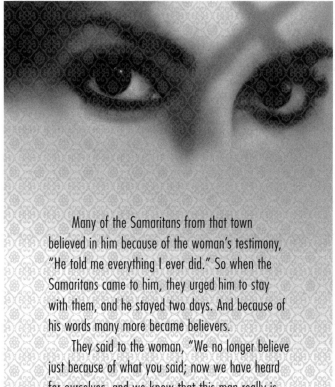

Many of the Samaritans from that town
believed in him because of the woman's testimony,
"He told me everything I ever did." So when the
Samaritans came to him, they urged him to stay
with them, and he stayed two days. And because of
his words many more became believers.

They said to the woman, "We no longer believe
just because of what you said; now we have heard
for ourselves, and we know that this man really is
the Savior of the world." (John 4:39–42 NIV)

Thirst is powerful.

Several years ago, I regularly played hockey in the evenings with a bunch of other middle-aged guys whose bodies could no longer do what their minds remembered they had once done.

It was during those games that I really experienced thirst. Even though I could bring a bottle of water to drink during the game, I never did. You see, I've got a bit of a hang-up about bacteria.

If you have ever watched a hockey game on television, you've seen the guys taking a big swig then spitting it out on the floor. That just creeps me right out, all that spitting near the water bottles. To make matters worse, some guys would drink out of the nearest bottle no matter whose name was on it.

So I'd play the whole two hours without a drink of water, and at my age and physical condition, most of my fluids ended up draining out of my body as sweat. Everytime we went to the bench for a rest, the other guys would take great big gulps of water. As we got closer to the end of the game, watching those guys drink water became that much more torturous.

Once the game ended, my body used that powerful tool called thirst to demand those fluids be replenished. As I changed into my street clothes, I was forced to turn my thoughts to quenching that thirst.

My first order of business after getting dressed was the cold-drink dispenser. I plugged in my two dollars to get a bottle of that stuff that's 10 percent real juice, a bunch of other stuff I can't pronounce, and filtered water.

It was always with great anticipation I screwed off the cap and let that cold liquid slake my thirst. For those seconds while the liquid was flowing down my throat I felt nothing but sheer pleasure from banishing that craving.

And everything about the story of the woman at the well has to do with thirst.

Jesus was thirsty when he got to the well. Somehow he didn't carry enough water nor anything with which to get water out of the well.

Wait a minute—Jesus is God and he doesn't forget anything.

Oh, that's right. So if he didn't forget, he must've meant to end up at that well—thirsty—and with no way to draw water. Jesus came to meet the Samaritan woman I call Abigail.

The Scriptures say, "He needed to go through Samaria" (John 4:4).

Fact is, Samaria was the shortest route to Galilee but not the preferred route. The Jews and Samaritans liked each other about as much as Yankee and Mets fans like one another, maybe even less. Jews usually took the longer route through Perea just to avoid running into their backward cousins.[1]

Jesus deliberately took that route to meet that particular woman. Since the cultural norm at that time was that men didn't talk to woman in public at the best of times, never mind a Jewish man and a Samaritan woman, he had to have a reason to speak to her. The reason Jesus created was thirst.

Thirst was probably the only icebreaker Jesus

could use to initiate a conversation with her that wouldn't have caused Abigail to take off running.

No, anything Jesus said other than "may I have a drink?" would've been taken the wrong way. Thirst was what started to bridge the gap between a Jewish traveler and a Samaritan woman.

But Abigail had her suspicions. She asked, "How is it that You, being a Jew, ask a drink from me, a Samaritan woman?" (John 4:9).

It's as if she was uncertain of his motives. She might just as easily have said, "Where do you get off talking to me? Our people hate each other. What do you really want?"

I'm thinking a woman who has had five previous husbands and currently lives with a guy out of wedlock has two problems: (1) men are attracted to her, and (2) she makes bad choices when it comes to men. A request for water might be innocent enough, but I think Abigail wanted to clarify that's all he really wanted.

And clarify it Jesus did. He quickly took the conversation from water that quenches earthly thirsts to water that quenches spiritual thirst. Abigail probably thought he was nuts until he brought up the matter of the five husbands and the current live-in.

During the hockey game, I noticed thirst the most when I was on the bench. When I was on the ice, the intensity of the play took my mind off of it. Abigail was no different.

While occupied with the game of life, she managed to keep that spiritual thirst at the back of her mind.

When Jesus brought up the immorality of her life, it was as if a referee blew the whistle and stopped the game. Abigail suddenly realized just how spiritually thirsty she was, and there stood Jesus offering her living water.

Abigail's thirst was so strong it didn't take her long to figure out just exactly who stood there and what the stakes were. I believe Abigail's whole pathetic life led up to that one moment, because when God met that girl, he was planning to use her to carry water to a whole bunch of thirsty people, and only she could do it.

There is no doubt in my mind Abigail was the right girl for the job of bringing Christ to the Samaritans. Think about it for a moment. Exactly how was the Jewish carpenter going to reach the Samaritans? He couldn't just march into town and set up a tent meeting; these people hated Jews, especially Jews who told them their religion was wrong.

He needed an agent who could go into Samaria and tell the men that the Messiah, not just some thirsty Jew, was by Jacob's well.

Maybe he could've used a different woman. Which one? As the town hussy, Abigail would be the only woman who ever went to the well alone. The other women traveled in groups. Even if some of them were spiritually thirsty, in a group setting they'd never admit they wanted to hear what this guy had to say for fear of retribution from the group.

And let's say a few of those women got around their prejudice and listened to Jesus—then what? They'd go back to the city and tell whom? The men? Do you think men would've listened? Not to those women they wouldn't. Those women were wives and daughters, and no man during that time was going to listen to his wife and daughter. Women were closer to being property than people.

But Abigail was different. Abigail was pretty and popular with the guys.

How do I know she was pretty? Well, she had five husbands. If she had five husbands, she had either money or looks. If she had money, then a servant would've gone to the well. So I'm guessing she had looks.

But if she had looks, how did she end up with five husbands and a live-in? If she was so pretty, why didn't her first husband keep her?

Unfortunately, looks can carry a relationship only so far. Even relationally challenged men want more than just beauty in a relationship.

Thanks to easy divorce laws in Samaria, once a man tired of Abigail's looks and realized she didn't have much else going, he could cut her loose with ease. Abigail would have no choice but to move on to the next man who wanted to become her interim care provider—until he lost interest too.

So when we find Abigail at the well, we find a woman with a life as empty as her water bucket. The fact man number six hasn't married her indicates to me maybe her looks are even starting to fail. It wouldn't surprise me if her plan for that morning was to jump into the well, but Jesus got in the way.

There he stands, a man speaking words that wash over her thirsty soul. A man who's looking into her, not at her. A man who is listening. For the first time, Abigail was in love with a man who truly loved her back, loved her enough to die for her.

Abigail ran back to the city and told the women all about meeting the Messiah. Oh, wait a minute—I got that wrong. The Scriptures tell us she told the men. Abigail had no relationship with the women, only the men. If the gospel was to spread to Samaria, it would have to start with the men. And why did the men listen to Abigail?

Ever been in a mixed group of men and women and one woman is particularly attractive? She could be talking about knitting and the guys would appear interested.

Abigail didn't talk to these guys about knitting; she talked to them about something more profound: living water.

And these guys were thirsty too. They were Samaritans. Every day they had to put up with the barbs of their Jewish cousins that they worshipped in the wrong spot; that they got it all wrong; that they lived pagan lives.

And when Abigail dropped the bombshell that this man said the Jews didn't have the worship thing right either, that perked them right up. And I know exactly how they felt.

Years ago, I was junior accountant at an integrated forest-products company. We made everything from lumber to newsprint. My division did the accounting for the sawmills and logging operations.

I need to explain something first or this won't make sense. Logs become either lumber or wood chips. Chips come from the part of the log that isn't suitable for lumber. These chips go to a pulp mill to be broken down into pulp. This pulp is then made into newsprint.

Due to poor lumber markets, the sawmills were losing money. It was a depressing place to work. It was even more depressing when the pulp mill and paper mill accountants would rub it in that if it wasn't for the pulp and paper division, the whole company would fail.

I don't exactly remember how it came about, except I was griping about the drubbing we took at the hands of the pulp and paper guys. The sawmill accountant called me into his office.

This guy was an enigma. He smoked a lot, drank a lot, and didn't get a lot of respect. I think the only reason they didn't get rid of him was it cost less to keep him than fire him.

He showed me a detailed analysis of the true cost of wood chips if the sawmills weren't running. If the pulp and paper guys had to do the logging then chip the logs, the cost would be so high they'd lose money and go broke in three months.

The reality was that making most of the logs into lumber lowered the cost of the chips enough that the pulp and paper mills made money. Without us, they'd go broke.

Abigail did the same thing for the men. Armed with Jesus' words, she enlightened them that the Jews

were no better off than them. She probably repeated
Jesus' words to them.

> Woman, believe Me, the hour is coming
> when you will neither on this mountain, nor
> in Jerusalem, worship the Father. You wor-
> ship what you do not know; we know what
> we worship, for salvation is of the Jews. But
> the hour is coming, and now is, when the
> true worshipers will worship the Father in
> spirit and truth; for the Father is seeking
> such to worship Him. God *is* Spirit, and
> those who worship Him must worship in
> spirit and truth. (John 4:21–24)

"Hey," Abigail said, "it's not just us that are
wrong—it's the Jews, too. This whole nation is in trouble. It's time to quit the blame game and solve the
problem."

Those thirsty men headed out to the well to find
out about the living water. And they went right to the
source to find out for themselves. I have to chuckle at
the last verse of this passage.

> Then they said to the woman, "Now we
> believe, not because of what you said, for we
> ourselves have heard *Him* and we know that
> this is indeed the Christ, the Savior of the
> world." (John 4:42)

Poor Abigail, the one time she does something truly worthwhile in her life, the guys take the credit away from her. But somehow, I don't think Abigail minded because she'd had a good long drink at the well of living water, and she'd never thirst again.

I think when we get to heaven and go on the tour of the homes of the stars of the Bible, we'll see this magnificent mansion. Someone's going to say, "Whose house is that? Paul's?"

The angel tour guide will smile and say, "No, that belongs to the woman at the well. The woman who showed the Samaritans the way to living water."

Some child will ask, "Hey, what about those cottages? Who lives there?"

The angel will grin. "Those six cottages belong to the men who were in her life. Seems they were thirsty too."[2]

Thirst. It drives us to drink, but we always thirst again. We can ignore the thirst as long as we're busy doing something else, but eventually we have to deal with it.

We can temporarily quench spiritual thirst with this world's pleasures. A half-dozen beers will quench it until the next morning; then you have a dry tongue, a headache, and a thirst.

A new dress and a makeover will quench it until the dress goes into the closet and the makeup comes off. Then you'll see the real you in the mirror and struggle with the fact that the goddess of the night before doesn't exist, and no amount of makeup or clothing will bring her back.

Money will quench it, until you run out of things to buy and realize no one loves you, just your money.

Romantic relationships will quench it until your heart is broken so many times you feel completely empty, just as Abigail did.

After a horrendous beating, after being nailed to a cross, Jesus said, "I thirst!" (John 19:28).

He gave his life up shortly thereafter. He did it because his creation, the creation he loved, wandered in the desert with a thirst that couldn't be quenched. He died to give us living waters. He died so no matter what our place is in this world, we can drink deeply of his love, knowing that his love and nothing else satisfies our thirst.

6

A BOY COMES BACK

(Surprise)

Nessa held her son's hand and watched his shallow breathing. She looked up at the physician standing by the door. He looked away. Sitting next to her, waiting with her, was her friend Tova. No relatives were there, because Nessa had no one in the world but her son.

She leaned over her son and spoke quietly into his ear. "Liron. Fight. You must stay. I need you. I love you."

Liron's eyelids flickered open, and hope flickered in Nessa's heart. He looked at her for a moment, smiled, and then looked away. Liron sucked in a short breath; he exhaled a long, deathly gasp.

Nessa threw herself on her son and wailed. "Please, God—no! You took my husband—why do you have to take my son?"

Hands rested on her shoulders.

"Nessa, let the physician check him," Tova said.

She let Tova pull her away from Liron.

She watched as the physician searched Liron for life. Nessa's thoughts scrambled back to the day she first held Liron in her arms. She never thought she'd have children; he became their life's joy, and so they named him Liron.

She remembered how their newborn son slept on her chest that first day. She remembered feeling his little lungs suck in the breath of life. She remembered his warm little body warming her heart.

As he grew, Nessa used her arms to comfort him when he was sad. She held him when his father, her husband, died. She remembered feeling his wracked sobs while she tried to console him.

And this last time that she held Liron, she knew the beautiful spirit that was her son had left.

"He's gone," the physician said.

She turned and buried her face in Tova's shoulder.

All the while, she wailed in despair, Nessa felt strangely disconnected from the world. People came into the room, they prepared his body, they moved her about, and she felt like a sheep, just doing whatever the shepherd said.

Suddenly she realized she was out on the street, walking in the direction of the graveyard. People were joining in behind her. She looked over her shoulder, and neighbors were carrying Liron's body on a stretcher; her knees buckled and she collapsed.

Tova was beside her, helping her stand.

"Be strong," Tova said. "Be strong for him."

Nessa nodded and forced herself to walk to the city gates, but each step was an acknowledgment she'd lost her son, her very own flesh. Nessa's heart went cold with the brutal acceptance that her only reason for living was gone. Her tears dried up. She knew that for the rest of her life she'd just be a shell going through the motions until God chose to strike her down too.

She moved on, ever aware her son's lifeless body was being carried behind her. The dreams of holding grandchildren in her arms were now just phantoms. She'd grow old, her strength would fail, she wouldn't be able to work, and she'd rely on the charity of those she lived among. She'd die with no family around her bed.

Nessa bit her lip as tears threatened again. Her heart wasn't as dead as she thought. Her hope may have died, but the pain of loss beat strong within her breast. If God had any compassion at all, he'd strike her down before she had to watch her son put to rest. The agony and despair of Liron's passing slammed her so hard she dissolved into tears just before they reached the city gates.

Tova quickly knelt beside her, encouraging her to carry on, but Nessa had had enough. She couldn't go on; there was no reason to go on. She just turned into Tova's embrace and wept bitter tears.

"Don't cry," a man's voice said.

Nessa turned and looked up. A solidly built but plain-looking man stood over her (Isa. 53:2 KJV).

"I think that's Jesus," Tova whispered. "The prophet everyone's been talking about."

Jesus held her eyes as if he knew her, as if he'd always known her. Were his eyes moist? She couldn't tell through her own tears. His countenance seemed to change, almost as if he was angry — not angry at her, just angry.

He moved past her and touched the stretcher where Liron lay.

"Young man, get up!"

Nessa scrambled to her feet. This couldn't be happening, could it?

Liron sat up, and Nessa felt like lightning struck her. He was alive! Jesus spoke and her son was alive. Liron started speaking; he was looking around, calling for her.

Jesus took her son off the stretcher and gave him to her. Nessa grabbed him in her arms and praised God through her tears (Jesus' dialogue based on Luke 7:13–14 CEV).

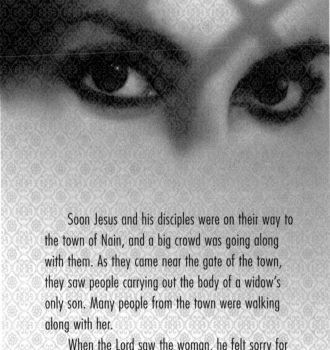

Soon Jesus and his disciples were on their way to the town of Nain, and a big crowd was going along with them. As they came near the gate of the town, they saw people carrying out the body of a widow's only son. Many people from the town were walking along with her.

When the Lord saw the woman, he felt sorry for her and said, "Don't cry!"

Jesus went over and touched the stretcher on which the people were carrying the dead boy. They stopped, and Jesus said, "Young man, get up!" The boy sat up and began to speak. Jesus then gave him back to his mother.

Everyone was frightened and praised God. They said, "A great prophet is here with us! God has come to his people."

News about Jesus spread all over Judea and everywhere else in that part of the country.
(Luke 7:11–17 CEV)

Surprise!

Surprise is a good word. We associate it with good times. Surprise is an unexpected birthday party, an unexpected Christmas gift, or perhaps an unexpected promotion at work. Surprises come during good times—unless of course God is the giver. God likes to surprise us, and he does his best work in our darkest hours.

On the day the widow of Nain's son died, God surprised everyone.

He surprised the socks off the crowd. To them it was just another funeral, not even a particularly good funeral. Anyone could tell just from looking at the widow of Nain that the after-party wouldn't be all that great. They'd be lucky to get water and bread. This funeral was just a distraction. It gave them something to fill their otherwise mundane day.

It would go like all the other funerals. A few words, a burial, a lot of crying. The smarter members of the crowd would slip away before someone got the bright idea of taking up a collection for the widow. After all, she wasn't really their problem, was she?

No, for this crowd this funeral would just be a status-quo funeral. No surprises for them—until ...

And what about this poor widow I call Nessa? In her grief-stricken mind, the concept of surprise didn't exist. She'd just lost the flesh of her flesh. She knew of no upside to death. The boy was gone; her reason for living was gone. She'd done the funeral thing before with her husband; she had no reason to expect anything different this time.

Her thoughts would've been charging back and forth between grief and wondering how she'd manage to survive without her son. The widow's procession was on its way out, and Jesus' group was on its way in. One group was going to have to step aside, so if the widow had seen Jesus and the crowd following him at all, they would've been a problem, not a surprise. Not a surprise—until …

Until Jesus came upon this funeral procession and "felt sorry" for the widow of Nain. Jesus saw her grief, her future, and felt sorry for her. And because he felt sorry for her, and because Jesus is God, he just decided to do something about it. He decided to give this poor widow an unfathomable surprise in her darkest hour.

With a touch on the stretcher, with some words from his mouth, Jesus yanked that boy back into the world of the living. He raised the widow's son from the dead. He surprised her in a way she never could've imagined.

With just those words, Jesus solved every problem running through the widow's head. With just those words, he took all her grief and pain away. A dark day suddenly filled with brilliant sunshine.

The crowd was astonished. We have to put this in perspective. In our modern world, we see people brought back from the dead all the time. With the medical science God in his grace has allowed us to develop, if we get there soon enough, almost any of us has a chance to bring someone back from the dead using CPR.

And paramedics have even more tools, such as

drugs and electroshock, to bring the dead back to life. Miracles involving bringing the dead back to life happen every day in our modern world.

But the day the widow of Nain's son died, the crowd had no concept of the dead coming back to life. So when Jesus touched that stretcher and spoke those words, they were more than surprised—they were awestruck.

Suddenly no one was thinking about whether cake would be served after the funeral, because there wasn't going to be a funeral! The Bible says,

> They were all filled with awe and praised God. "A great prophet has appeared among us," they said. "God has come to help his people." (Luke 7:16 NIV)

These people were living in dark times. The Romans ruled over them, and the Romans weren't nice rulers. The people lived in fear of beatings, imprisonment, and sometimes even death.

They had a heritage *from* God but no knowledge *of* God. Their spiritual leaders could only give them countless rules to earn salvation, but no hope of salvation. When Jesus raised that boy, he brought light into their world. He surprised them with hope.

It's in our darkest times that God finds his best opportunities to surprise us. It's when we're down that he can lift us up.

My wife and I had three children. All three children

were born premature, and the first two died. This is why I have such empathy for the widow of Nain. Regrettably, I can say with honesty, "I know what she went through."

But unlike the widow of Nain, I don't have a resurrection story. Our two sons died and they stayed dead. That's the experience of most of us. Tragedy strikes us, pounds us into the ground, and overwhelms us with despair. The idea of God surprising us during those times almost sounds ludicrous. But during the birth of our first son, Michael, surprise us he did.

We'd just moved to Vancouver Island for work. We didn't have a family doctor yet, and my wife, Mary, went into labor.

We were brand-new Christians without a church home. We had no grounding in our newly found faith, and to add insult to injury, I lost the job I came to Vancouver Island to get. At the time, it didn't seem like God cared much for our plight.

The first surprise came at the hospital. The attending doctor immediately started Mary on drugs to stop the labor, but he didn't hold out much hope of being successful.

The local hospital just wasn't equipped to deal with premature babies. The cold facts were if the baby were born there, he would die. We had to get to Vancouver, which meant a long drive, a ferry ride, and another long drive. The doctor told us we didn't have that kind of time. Mary would be giving birth on the journey if we tried it.

But God stepped in with a surprise.

The doctor covering emergency that day was also the regular doctor for the local military airbase. Just like Jesus was moved with compassion for the widow of Nain, God moved that doctor to have compassion for us.

He made a phone call to his buddy at the airbase, pulled a few strings, and shortly thereafter a military helicopter landed at the hospital. Moments later, we were whisked across the Georgia strait to the B.C. Children's Hospital in Vancouver.

At the hospital, we went through a roller coaster of emotions as they tried to stop the labor. They failed, and Michael was born just shy of two pounds. The little guy defied the odds and made it past the crucial first twenty-four hours. He continued to beat the odds until he was stabilized.

Our next challenge was that we were running out of cash. We had no church family to call on. We just couldn't afford to stay there any longer. We had to go home.

Home wasn't much either. We lived in a little travel trailer at a campground. The campground gave us a good deal because it was the off-season, but money was still short.

We tried to supplement our unemployment-insurance benefits by selling firewood. One particular day, with thoughts of our son struggling in the hospital on our minds, we set out to cut up some logs. The day didn't go well.

We had two chain saws. The first tree I started to cut down fell backward and pinched the saw blade. I couldn't pull it out, but that was no problem. I got my second chain saw to cut above the pinched blade. I pulled the cord and it wouldn't start. I yanked on that cord until my arm trembled from exhaustion. It wouldn't start no matter what I tried.

Finally, I resorted to the tried-and-true method of tree cutting—I hacked it down with an axe and retrieved my other chain saw. We were beaten. Chain saw number one had a broken blade, chain saw number two wouldn't start, and my arms were rubber from pulling the cord and chopping at that tree.

We packed up and went home.

Moments after we arrived home, the phone rang. The doctor said Michael had taken a turn for the worse, and we should prepare ourselves. Fifteen minutes later, he called to say Michael had passed away. God had surprised us again.

Surprise! What kind of surprise is that?

God allowed that day's events to happen so we wouldn't come home to find a message that our child had died. He wanted us to have time to pray and prepare, so he sent us home early. We cried plenty that day and the days thereafter.

I didn't handle the grief well. I kind of fell apart trying to understand why God would go to such great lengths to give Michael a shot at life, only to let him die. God surprised me by telling me the story of David. David went through what I went through.

David's son fell ill soon after he was born. David prayed for that son, he fasted for that son, and God still let the child die (2 Sam. 12:16–23).

God gave us the time to pray for our son, but in his wisdom, he chose not to heal him. Like David's child, our son died. But when David learned his child had died, he didn't fall into depression; he did something totally unexpected.

> And he said, "While the child was alive, I fasted and wept; for I said, 'Who can tell *whether* the LORD will be gracious to me, that the child may live?' But now he is dead; why should I fast? Can I bring him back again? I shall go to him, but he shall not return to me." (2 Sam. 12:22–23)

God surprised me by making sure I knew that our son was safe, he was within God's plan, and everything would work out. Was that surprise, that knowledge, enough to stop my mourning? Of course not. But what that surprise, what that knowledge did, was let me feel his love in my mourning.

It's a forgone conclusion that we'll have grief on this earth. It's also a forgone conclusion that Jesus will be with us throughout that grief. When he sees us in our pain he has compassion on us. He won't necessarily raise our children from the dead, but he will look for opportunities to surprise us with his love and grace by easing our burdens, by carrying it for us.

When you've been hit so hard you just don't think you can get back up, make sure you open your eyes. Open your eyes so you can be surprised by the hand of

Jesus reaching down to help you up and through whatever you are experiencing.

7

AN UNUSUAL DINNER GUEST

(Blindness)

"Is that Jesus?"

Simon the Pharisee turned and smiled at his friend Abner, who had just settled himself in beside him. "It is."

"Why is he here? You realize he's not exactly popular back in Jerusalem?"

Simon nodded. "I've heard he's stepped on a few toes."

"Aren't you worried that this gets back to Caiaphas?"

"What gets back?"

"That you had that blasphemer in your home, eating with you and your guests."

"I like to judge a man for myself. If he's a blasphemer, I'm sure we'll know soon enough."

But Simon wasn't seeing the evidence of blasphemy as soon as he'd like. Jesus seemed to restrict his conversation to safe topics with those guests who would talk to him. And when no one would talk to him, Jesus seemed content to recline and enjoy the food Simon provided. Nothing was going right.

A servant approached, dropped to his knee, and leaned close to Simon.

"Yes," the Pharisee said.

"There's a woman outside wanting to come in and see Jesus."

"What kind of woman?"

The servant leaned closer and whispered so only Simon could hear. "She's one of the harlots."

Simon smiled. "Really?"

"Should I chase her away?"

"No. Let her in," Simon said, and waved the servant away.

"What was that about?" Abner said.

"I think we're going to get the show I hoped for."

"What's that supposed to mean?"

"Just watch," Simon said.

Shortly thereafter, the woman entered the dining area. All the guests stopped eating and went silent at her presence. She looked about and her eyes stopped on Jesus, who was facing away from her.

"I think that's one of the harlots," Abner said. "Why did you let her in?"

"She's here to see Jesus."

"Well, this should be interesting." Abner sat up and looked at the woman. "There's something different about her."

"She's not dressed like a harlot," Simon said.

"Yes, that's right," Abner said. "Must not be working right now. Too bad. Still, Jesus and this kind of woman—that would be of interest to Jerusalem."

"It sure would," Simon said.

The woman approached Jesus from behind, and he continued eating as if he hadn't noticed the room had gone silent.

She stood over him, her eyes fixed on the back of Jesus head. Her eyes moistened and the woman threw herself at Jesus' feet. Tears streamed down her cheeks and dropped onto Jesus' feet. Simon sat up, not believing what he was seeing.

His mouth hung open when she used her long raven hair to wipe the tears off Jesus' feet. The only sound in the dining chamber was the woman sobbing.

Abner stood. "Simon, I can't be here with this going on. I must go."

Simon was so mesmerized by the bizarre display in front of him he didn't even acknowledge his friend's departure.

He sucked in a short breath as the woman started to kiss Jesus' feet, then poured perfume on them. "If this man really were a prophet, he would know what kind of woman is touching him! He would know that she is a sinner."

Jesus looked over at him. "Simon, I have something to say to you."

Simon straightened. He hadn't spoken loud enough for anyone to hear, and yet Jesus had heard. "Teacher, what is it?"

Jesus told him, "Two people were in debt to a moneylender. One of them owed him five hundred silver coins, and the other owed him fifty. Since neither of them could pay him back, the moneylender said that they didn't have to pay him anything. Which one of them will like him more?"

Simon rubbed his chin. What kind of question was this? Was Jesus trying to trick him? Everyone in the room looked at him to see how he'd answer. He decided the obvious answer would be the best. "I suppose it would be the one who had owed more and didn't have to pay it back."

His guests shifted their attention to Jesus.

"You are right," Jesus said.

He turned toward the woman and said to Simon, "Have you noticed this woman? When I came into your home, you didn't give me any water so I could wash my feet. But she has washed my feet with her tears and dried them with her hair. You didn't greet me with a kiss, but from the time I came in, she has not stopped kissing my feet. You didn't even pour olive oil on my head, but she has poured expensive perfume on my feet. So I tell you that all her sins are forgiven, and that is why she has shown great love. But anyone who has been forgiven for only a little will show only a little love."

Then Jesus said to the woman, "Your sins are forgiven." (Dialogue of Jesus and Simon is based on Luke 7:39–48 CEV.)

The Pharisee who had invited Jesus saw this and said to himself, "If this man really were a prophet, he would know what kind of woman is touching him! He would know that she is a sinner."

Jesus said to the Pharisee, "Simon, I have something to say to you."

"Teacher, what is it?" Simon replied.

Jesus told him, "Two people were in debt to a moneylender. One of them owed him five hundred silver coins, and the other owed him fifty. Since neither of them could pay him back, the moneylender said that they didn't have to pay him anything. Which one of them will like him more?"

Simon answered, "I suppose it would be the one who had owed more and didn't have to pay it back."

"You are right," Jesus said.

He turned toward the woman and said to Simon, "Have you noticed this woman? When I came into your home, you didn't give me any water so I could wash my feet. But she has washed my feet with her tears and dried them with her hair. You didn't greet me with a kiss, but from the time I came in, she has not stopped kissing my feet. You didn't even pour olive oil on my head, but she has poured expensive perfume on my feet. So I tell you that all her sins are forgiven, and that is why she has shown great love. But anyone who has been forgiven for only a little will show only a little love." Then Jesus said to the woman, "Your sins are forgiven." (Luke 7:39–48 CEV)

I was in total blindness. I had to rely on my senses of touch and hearing, and I didn't have much time because someone was calling for help.

I felt around on all fours until I found a wall. It didn't help that some people were laughing at my plight and making it difficult to hear the person calling to me to find them.

Standing up just wasn't an option. I didn't know where I started from, so I had no idea what obstacles I might hit. Another call for help heightened the sense of urgency.

Following the wall, I eventually came to a door. More laughter echoed from behind me. It sounded like the call came from behind the door, so I pushed it open and crawled on through. Now even the person calling for help was giggling. I found a foot. The exercise was over.

Someone helped pull the opaque plastic bag off of my head. Next, I pulled the mask of the Scott Airpack off and looked at the grinning victim who sat on the washroom floor.

Had this been a real fire, the victim probably would've died. But it was just a practice exercise at my local fire hall where I was a volunteer. We trained blind because when there's fire, there's smoke—so much smoke you can't see much of anything, so you need to rely on all your other senses to navigate through a burning building.

In this world, though, many of us suffer from blindness. The building is on fire all around us, and because of the smoke, we're blind and can't find a way out. Because of this blindness, either we stumble through the building until something falls on us, or we fall through a hole in the floor.

The only way to gain sight in a smoke-filled building is if the firefighters vent it. They chop holes in strategic places in the building to allow the smoke to escape. Once they vent the smoke, the chances of rescue increase significantly.

At that banquet where the woman washed Jesus' feet, two people saw the same man and came to drastically different conclusions. One saw him through smoke and the other saw him clearly.

Let's deal with the blind guy first. That would be Simon. He wasn't totally blind because he had some inkling that Jesus wasn't just your run-of-the-mill teacher. Otherwise, he wouldn't have invited him to the banquet.

But he also didn't give Jesus the full courtesy due a teacher. He didn't give Jesus any water to wash his feet. One commentator speculates the whole purpose of Simon's invitation to Jesus was to trick him.[1] Jesus was there to be the entertainment. And entertain Jesus did, although Simon's blindness prevented him from really seeing the show.

All Simon could see through the smoke of his sinfulness was a woman of ill repute washing Jesus' feet with her hair. Not once did he ask himself just what did Jesus do to make this otherwise hardened woman a blubbering mess of emotions.

Simon commented, "If this man really were a prophet, he would know what kind of woman is touching him! He would know that she is a sinner" (Luke 7:39 CEV).

Obviously Simon knew what kind of woman she was. Didn't he think it strange that a woman who made her living selling her attention and affections was throwing it away on the feet of this "prophet"? Simon's blindness prevented him from seeing the complete and utter change in this woman's life. This change should've been like the firefighters venting the building so the smoke of ignorance could clear enough for Simon to see the way of escape.

Strange as it seems, some people resist being rescued. Hysteria overcomes them, and like panicked horses, they do everything but the smart thing in a fire. In this case, once the smoke cleared, Simon simply closed his eyes.

So the light went looking for Simon. Jesus told this Pharisee the parable of two debtors to help Simon understand that great sin leads to great forgiveness, which leads to great love. The Scriptures don't indicate whether Simon ever got the point on more than a superficial level. Staying in a burning building is a terrible thing.

The woman, though—she got it. Many speculate on who she might have been: maybe Mary Magdalene, maybe the woman caught in the act of adultery. Who she was really isn't important. What's important is she lived a wicked, sinful life. There's a tendency in modern media to glorify prostitution. There is nothing to glorify.

Just like prostitutes today, prostitutes back then were abused and had no social standing. Unlike today, the women back then lived in constant fear of a harsh law. In today's culture there are just too many TV shows portraying prostitution as a legitimate, even fun occupation. In this woman's day, the whole culture was permeated with religion that daily reminded her she was a prostitute.

I'm speculating that one day she crossed Jesus' path. Maybe he confronted her with harsh words, maybe he called her to repent, or maybe he confronted her with kind words and showed her that God loved her, that she wasn't just something to be sold, but someone to love.

I'm thinking she might not have really understood what happened right away. She'd lived in the blindness of sin for many years. Suddenly, this pinprick of light called her from that darkness. Jesus moved on, but she kept following that pinprick of light until it became brighter than the rising sun.

Once she was totally in that light, she looked behind her and saw the building of her former life. She saw a building fully engulfed in flames, with smoke pouring out of the roof where Jesus had chopped a hole to vent the smoke of her life. A sweat probably broke out on her forehead as she realized how close to eternal torment she came.

Then she thought of that man, the man who opened her eyes, who took her blindness away. He went into that burning building of her life, threw her on his shoulder, and carried her to safety. He rescued her.

Before, this woman would sell her love to any man who would pay for it. Now she wanted to give her love to the man who wanted nothing more than her love. When the light went on for this woman, she knew exactly who Jesus was, and she showered him with utter devotion.

She didn't care what the other people in the crowd thought. She didn't care that her business was now ruined. Her soul yearned to express to her creator her love for his gift to her.

It's ironic that the "sinner" figured out who Jesus was, and the "righteous" Pharisee decided to stay in his burning building. The question for us today is: Which of those two are we?

I'm a professional accountant, and one of the functions of my profession is to audit financial statements. In a nutshell our job is to do our accountant thing so we can report on the reliability of a company's financial statements. One tool we use when we audit is a checklist. It's simply a form that lists all the tests and questions to consider when looking at different parts of the financial accounts. These checklists are very useful, provided you use the right checklist.

You see, audits aren't the only things accountants can do to a statement. Sometimes we review them. A review is nowhere near as detailed as an audit and doesn't give the same confidence the statements are right.

And then there's what we call a Notice to Reader. This is a very bare-bones examination of the statement, and we make it pretty clear to anyone relying on these statements that we make no representation as to whether they're right or not.

Imagine if an accountant used the Notice to Reader checklist for an audit. What a mess that would make! People would read financial statements thinking the accountant has done an in-depth analysis, not realizing they could be completely wrong. These people might invest in the business only to lose their money if the statements were completely wrong.

Do you know what happens to a professional accountant who uses the wrong checklist? They don't get to be a professional accountant any longer.

But people are using the wrong checklist every day. They're using the "I'm basically a good person" checklist. The "I do more good than bad" checklist. This is the wrong checklist to use to measure your life. It's a checklist of deeds.

I'm good because

- I give to charity.
- I've never killed anyone.
- I go to church.
- I never cheated on my wife.
- I let my neighbor use my ladder.
- I mostly tell the truth on my taxes.
- if my good deeds are put on the scale of life, they will more than outweigh the bad deeds. I'm going to heaven!

The problem with this checklist is it isn't Jesus' checklist. This checklist is like sitting in a bathtub of water in a burning building and thinking if you stay underwater and hold your breath long enough the fire won't get you. Once the building gets hot enough, the water will boil!

The good deeds versus bad deeds checklist is completely wrong.

Take my checklist for example. Did I say something
about having never murdered? Jesus' checklist says,

> You have heard that it was said to those of
> old, *"You shall not murder,* and whoever
> murders will be in danger of the judgment."
> But I say to you that whoever is angry with
> his brother without a cause shall be in dan-
> ger of the judgment. And whoever says to
> his brother, "Raca!" shall be in danger of the
> council. But whoever says, "You fool!" shall
> be in danger of hell fire. (Matt. 5:21–22)

Ouch! Jesus equates anger with my brother as the
same as murder. That wasn't in the good deeds versus
bad deeds checklist.

I think I did say something about never having
cheated on my wife. The Jesus checklist says,

> You have heard that it was said to those of
> old, *"You shall not commit adultery."* But I
> say to you that whoever looks at a woman to
> lust for her has already committed adultery
> with her in his heart. (Matt. 5:27–28)

Yikes! I'm not sure I like that interpretation of
adultery at all. Maybe I should be like Simon and close

my eyes before I find anything more I've done wrong. Too late. Jesus has already started venting the burning building of my life.

The apostle Paul writes,

> Do you not know that the unrighteous will not inherit the kingdom of God? Do not be deceived. Neither fornicators, nor idolaters, nor adulterers, nor homosexuals, nor sodomites, nor thieves, nor covetous, nor drunkards, nor revilers, nor extortioners will inherit the kingdom of God. (1 Cor. 6:9–10)

I'm beginning to feel like the woman who washed Jesus' feet. Suddenly I can see the building is on fire all around me. But how will I escape? Who will guide me out?

I'm glad the apostle Paul finished the previous quote with this:

> And such were some of you. But you were washed, but you were sanctified, but you were justified in the name of the Lord Jesus and by the Spirit of our God. (1 Cor. 6:11)

Through his sacrifice on the cross, Jesus made a way for us to escape our blindness. He vented the burning building of the smoke so we could see, then he came in after us.

And know this. In real life—versus TV life—firefighters don't go charging into burning buildings if the structure is unstable and about to come down on them. It's safety first with them as well. They have rules and procedures to follow and will let you die if they can't rescue you within those rules and procedures.

But unlike a human firefighter, Jesus will charge into any burning building to get you—even if it ends up killing him. Jesus will find you, he will carry you, and he will never drop you. Once you acknowledge to him the true state of your life, nothing will stop him from getting to you. The flames of our sin can be as high as the heavens, as deep as the sea, and he will sweep them away with his grace.

There's nothing you've done, nothing you could do, that can keep Jesus from saving you if you repent. And after he's lifted you off his shoulder and placed you safely on the ground, you might just want to look back at the burning building you once lived in.

When you see the flames consuming that old structure, a cold sweat might break out on your forehead when you realize where you used to live. You just might find yourself dropping to the ground in front of the one who saved you. You might even feel driven to wash his feet with your hair, all the while sobbing uncontrollably. Blindness is a terrible thing; let him open your eyes.

8

THE LAST RESORT

(DESPERATION)

Helen grimaced with every thrash of her daughter's body. Cloths bound her child's wrists and ankles to the corners of the bed. Blood seeping from the chafed skin stained the bindings.

Cassie opened her mouth and let loose one of her guttural screams, then broke into a tirade of curses at Helen.

How did this happen? Just a month ago, Cassie was a young girl full of life, giggling with her friends and showing more than casual interest in the boys. Now she was some beast that had to be restrained, a beast that tried to bite Helen's hand when she fed it.

Helen buried her face in her hands and wept. She knew the answer to her own question. She'd let Cassie run with the older teens. They'd found an idol of one of the gods and started to worship it. Like the other adults, Helen never thought much of it. She thought it was just childish play. Like the other adults, she had no idea how far the children had gone.

Bowing to the thing only amused Cassie and her friends for so long, but it wasn't until animals started disappearing that anyone realized they were sacrificing to it. Shortly after that, her daughter changed. She became quiet, rebellious.

Helen tried to keep Cassie from the idol, but her daughter would escape at night and run to worship it. One morning Cassie came back, her clothes torn, drool dripping down her cheek. That morning Cassie tried to kill her.

The physician gave Cassie medicines to calm her, and they worked for a short while. But it wasn't long before they didn't calm the beast her daughter had become. After that, the physician tried more painful methods to force the demon out of her child; those methods only seemed to delight it.

Finally, the physician gave up. His suggestion was for her to put Cassie out of her misery quietly and quickly finish the work the idol had started. He had some medicines she could use.

Helen kept the medicines. Just a couple of nights ago — an especially horrible night when Cassie frothed blood and her muscles strained to the point of breaking the restraints — Helen began to feel as though there was no way out. She'd have no choice but to kill her child.

That night she put the poison to her daughter's lips. Cassie's eyes opened and searched hers. For a brief second her child looked back at her, and then the eyes turned to those of an animal. The animal grinned, then dared her to do it, to kill her child.

Helen threw the medicine across the room then fled to her own sleeping quarters with the creature's cackling chasing after her. The night tormented her as the horrible realization of what she'd almost done sank in. She ran outside, looked at the sky, and begged that if anyone were listening they'd show her a way out, a way that didn't include killing Cassie.

The next morning a neighbor came over. Her husband, a merchant, had just returned from Galilee. He told her a fantastic tale about a Jewish prophet heading toward their country. A prophet who'd healed the blind, cured leprosy, raised the dead … and … cast out demons. A prophet they called Jesus. A prophet some of the Jewish people were claiming was their Messiah.

The Jews referred to her people as dogs and thought they were superior, but Helen didn't care. If there were any hope at all, she would find this Jewish prophet and do whatever it took to get him to come to her daughter.

Helen washed her daughter's face, ignoring the beast's attempts to bite her. She tried to feed Cassie, but the beast wouldn't let her child take any food. She checked the bindings to make sure they'd hold while she went to find this Jesus.

It tore at her heart to leave her child alone, but none of the neighbors would dare stay with the child. She put her hand on Cassie's forehead.

"Cassie, if you can hear me, forgive me. I have to leave you alone for a while."

Cassie — no, the beast — cursed her. It promised to kill her child while she was gone.

Helen's tears fell on Cassie's face. "I'll be back as soon as I can. I just need to find this Jesus."

Cassie's body arched and the creature howled. What was it Helen saw in the creature's eyes? Fear. Yes, she saw fear.

Helen took a deep breath, stood, and went to find Jesus, the prophet whose name struck fear in the demon that held her daughter.

Her neighbor's husband had passed Jesus on his way back. He said Jesus seemed to be heading toward the coast. And after an exhausting journey, that's where Helen found him.

He had people around him; he looked tired. Helen was tired as well, tired from the journey, but the thought of Cassie all alone, tormented by that beast, pushed her forward.

She rushed toward Jesus and cried out. "Lord, Son of David, have mercy on me! My daughter is suffering terribly from demon possession."

Jesus made no sign he heard her. Instead, he moved away from her. With visions of Cassie's tormented face in her mind, Helen kept pace with him, calling out to Jesus. She'd keep calling until he acknowledged her, until he saved her daughter.

He had men with him. Helen started to yell at them, to beg them to get their master to help her. They went to him, they said some words, and he stopped and looked at her.

Helen stumbled toward him and fell to her knees. With tears rolling down her cheeks, she implored him, "Lord, help me!"

He looked at her as if she was some kind of stranger. As if she had no business being there. He looked at her with disdain.

Finally he spoke. "It is not right to take the children's bread and toss it to their dogs."

That's it! Her daughter would be destroyed by this demon just because she wasn't a Jew! That just wasn't good enough. Cassie had to be set free, and this Jewish prophet could do it.

His expression changed. He looked at her as if waiting for an answer. Suddenly Helen had a thought.

"Yes, Lord," she said, "but even the dogs eat the crumbs that fall from their masters' table."

A grin broke across his face. Were his eyes moist? She couldn't tell from the blur of her tears.

"Woman, you have great faith! Your request is granted."

He turned and walked away from her. (Dialogue based on Matt. 15:22–28 NIV.)

Helen watched him go with her mouth hanging open. Her request was granted? That's all he had to do to rid her daughter of those vile vermin?

Helen grinned. Of course that's all he had to do. The Jews talked about the Messiah all the time; the Messiah came directly from God. He didn't have to see Cassie; he didn't have to touch her; he just had to speak.

Joy overcame Helen's exhaustion. She walked, giving no thought to the pain in her feet, the aching in her legs. Jesus had spoken. She had to get back to Cassie.

Walking through the night, Helen returned home. She entered the house and was struck by the silence. Cassie wasn't screaming any more. Helen rushed to her daughter's room.

Tears welled up in her eyes. Her daughter's chest gently rose and fell with each breath of restful sleep. Helen rushed to Cassie's side and dropped beside her. She reached for one of the cloths that bound her daughter's wrists and her hand went to her mouth. There was no sign of the chafing.

Cassie's eyes fluttered open. "Mother. Where have you been?"

Helen wrapped her daughter in her arms and answered with her sobs of joy.

Leaving that place, Jesus withdrew to the region of Tyre and Sidon. A Canaanite woman from that vicinity came to him, crying out, "Lord, Son of David, have mercy on me! My daughter is suffering terribly from demon-possession."

Jesus did not answer a word. So his disciples came to him and urged him, "Send her away, for she keeps crying out after us."

He answered, "I was sent only to the lost sheep of Israel."

The woman came and knelt before him. "Lord, help me!" she said.

He replied, "It is not right to take the children's bread and toss it to their dogs."

"Yes, Lord," she said, "but even the dogs eat the crumbs that fall from their masters' table."

Then Jesus answered, "Woman, you have great faith! Your request is granted." And her daughter was healed from that very hour. (Matt. 15:21–28 NIV)

Ever hear someone say, "I'm desperate for a cup of coffee"? They're not desperate. They won't die if they don't get that coffee. The worst that will happen is they'll get a caffeine headache.

The woman I call Helen was desperate.

Her child was afflicted in a way she couldn't understand or help.

Like any parent, she probably turned to the traditional solution: physicians. And they probably tried the usual methods, then some not-so-usual methods. By the time they were done, Helen would feel like a cornered rabbit with nowhere to turn.

Helen was right where Jesus wanted her.

In a recent sermon, my pastor said God does his best work when people are desperate. If the physicians could have managed the girl's condition, Helen never would've sought out Jesus. It was that complete and utter hopelessness caused by desperation that made her turn to Jesus.

And turning to Jesus would've been a big deal. She was a Canaanite; Canaanites didn't like Jews, and vice versa. Jesus was not just a Jew; he was a big-name Jew. Getting to him would be a long shot at best, and expecting help from him would be an even longer shot—but what else could she do?

So desperation drove that woman to Jesus. And Jesus did what no human being could do. He made her daughter whole again. Through Helen's desperation, Jesus sent the first indication that salvation wasn't only for the Jews, but for the Gentiles, too. Helen's desperation gave hope to her people.

One of the greatest barriers between God and us is pride. Pride is touted around as a virtue. The coach tells his team to have pride in itself. The boss tells workers to have pride in the company. The world tells you to have pride in yourself when you can stand on your own two feet. But God says, "Lean on me."

Unfortunately, pride often gets between God and what he wants to do in us. So don't be surprised when you find yourself meeting desperation someday, because desperation crushes pride any day of the week.

After our son died, my wife and I moved back to the Revelstoke area. We lived in a valley inhabited by maybe fifty people. It was also where we both had found Christ a year before. It was also the worst possible place for two new Christians to be.

We got saved in that area through Christian comic books, but we were discipled by people who had some pretty strange ideas. One of those ideas was that the "whore" of Babylon mentioned in Revelation 17 (KJV) actually referred to the established church. You know, churches like the one where you go, with a pastor who faithfully preaches God's Word each Sunday.

God needed to get us out of there, but we just wouldn't go. We were filled with pride that not only had we found God, but also we'd found "truth." We knew something that millions of other Christians didn't—the church was the whore. We became spiritually proud.

We didn't want to leave the valley. We had a sweetheart deal where we could live essentially free in a cabin on twenty acres of forested land. It didn't have water or power, but it helped us hide from the "world." Part of the "world" was work, and somehow I got it in my mind that the less I got involved with the "world" the better—so I didn't go back to work.

We were quite content to live on unemployment-insurance benefits with the rest of the quasi hippies in the valley. We attributed the fact that we had started arguing to Satan's trying to drive us out of the valley rather than to our being isolated and without fellowship.

And that's when God allowed circumstances to throw us into desperation.

It was winter. In Revelstoke winter means snow—lots of it. Snowbanks higher than most pickup trucks lined the highway. Late one night, we were traveling down the highway to a friend's home when we saw a truck nose first into the snowbank. We started to slow down when we realized the truck was occupied by the local "crazy" and a couple of his friends.

This guy had spent time in prison and had a reputation for being highly unpredictable when drunk. The way he staggered and waved, he looked drunk. The prospect of being alone with him and two of his equally drunk buddies on a dark highway late at night frightened us, so we just kept on going.

When he got out of that snowbank, he tracked us down to our friend's place and immediately assaulted me. The only reason he backed off at all is our friend grabbed his rifle.

Now, I grew up in a nice, middle-class suburb. I

had no experience with anything like this. Mary and I were terrified. On his way out the door, this guy threatened to kill us next time he saw us.

We called the police, and they tracked him down and charged him with impaired driving. As for the threat, they told us there was little they could do if he carried it out due to our isolated location and the lack of a telephone. (Cell phones were the stuff of science fiction back then.) Their best advice: Get out of the area.

So we headed back to the cabin, packed up everything we could, and threw it in the back of our pickup truck. Then we headed west to Salmon Arm with fifty dollars in our pocket.

We never thought of going to our families for help. First, they were part of the "world." They weren't Christians. Second, they probably wouldn't help anyway. Somehow my parents got it in their minds that we were part of some cult by the way we talked about the "whore of Babylon" and how we'd found the only truth. Boy, I can't figure out how they came to that conclusion!

But Canada is a great country when it comes to being broke. No one starves here unless they've got some kind of substance-abuse problem.

We went to the local welfare office and explained that I had spent my whole unemployment-insurance check on groceries the day before, that some guy had threatened to kill us, and that we had no money for a place to stay.

The caseworker checked out our story and said it

would be no problem. He told us to find a place to rent and he'd send the check directly to the landlord.

We looked for a place to rent, but we couldn't find anything available in that town for the amount welfare was willing to pay. Needless to say, we were starting to get worried.

We backtracked to a town called Sicamous, just east of Salmon Arm, hoping its more isolated location would mean cheaper rents. We never got a chance to find out.

We were stopped just outside the Sicamous police station, planning our next move, when our worst fear walked out of the front door—the man who'd threatened to kill us. He looked up and it seemed like he saw us.

We hit the gas and headed the only direction left to us—south. Now we were worried.

The next major population center is called Vernon. We went to the welfare office and got the nicest lady you could ever meet for our caseworker. She nodded her head at the right points in our story, raised her eyebrows in concern at our plight, and promised to do what she could. We started to relax.

The lady left her office, was gone for fifteen minutes, then came back. She'd checked out our story, talked to her supervisor, and was sorry to inform us we weren't eligible for any help because the amount of unemployment insurance I had received the day before was greater than the amount they paid recipients.

To say we were shocked was an understatement.

What about the other welfare office, we asked? He said we were eligible. She just smiled and told us he was wrong and there was nothing they could do.

I looked at her and said, "What can we do? We can't go back to Revelstoke."

She shrugged and suggested we try the Salvation Army.

Now Jesus had us exactly where he wanted us.

With little money, nowhere to stay, and no government to help us out, we were—desperate!

Reluctantly we found the Salvation Army and entered the building we'd been taught was a part of the great whore of Babylon. God had been herding us there from the moment I chose not to stop for that guy stuck in the snowbank—and desperation was the shepherd that did the herding.

We met with the Salvation Army family-resource worker. He was a stern-looking man whose expression offered little hope of meaningful help. We told him our saga, and his face never betrayed any indication whether he believed us or not. We found out later he didn't even bother to check out our story.

He asked us if we went to church—no. He asked if we were married—yes. He asked when my next unemployment check would arrive—two weeks. He then gave us a two-week voucher for a local motel with no strings attached. All he did is mention services were on Sunday and we were welcome to attend.

How could we not attend? In our greatest need, this church helped us out. At least we owed them a look. And when we went to church that Sunday, we were shocked.

The music was lively, the pastor preached from the Bible, and there were no indications this place was a member of the whore of Babylon. It was a place of Christian people worshipping Christ and trying to love one another as best as they could. Thanks to desperation, God finally got us on the path of our Christian walk where we could grow and learn of him.

Jesus met the lady I called Helen at her point of desperation. All those circumstances that penned her in were really shepherding her to him. Jesus didn't cause Helen's daughter to be demon possessed. He didn't flood her life with evil—someone else did that. But he used those circumstances to do a great work in Helen's life.

If you love Christ and find yourself in desperate circumstances, stop for a moment and pray. Ask him what it is he's trying to do with your desperation.

He might be trying to make you grow, as he did in our case. He might be using those desperate circumstances so you'll drop to your knees in prayer and call out, "Lord, help me!" (Matt. 15:25 NIV).

It's sad but true: We do some of our best praying and worshipping during desperate times. Maybe Jesus is using those desperate circumstances to get you to talk to him. He misses your company, and he'll take advantage of anything to get you back into fellowship with him.

Sometimes Jesus uses your desperation to reach others.

Even after we got involved in a local church and began growing in Christ, a crisis still came our way.

Our daughter was also born premature. We still ended up in desperate circumstances—only this time, we had people walking with us.

Church members offered us their help while we had to stay in Vancouver. The local Salvation Army chaplain often prayed over our daughter's incubator and counseled and loved us. Our desperate circumstances weren't so much for our growth as for those people who watched us. They learned about Jesus by how we handled our desperation.

All I can tell you is my wife and I have been in desperate circumstances various times throughout our lives, and each of those times, Jesus met us. If you're in desperate circumstances, pray to him.

Pray to him about everything you can. God is your father. If you've ever watched a toddler babble at her parents, notice how they'll sit and listen to every single word and sound. So go ahead and babble at God. Tell him what you want, tell him what you need, tell him how you feel, tell him you're desperate—desperate for him to help.

Then wait. Wait to see how he works things out. It may not be the way you want, but it will be the way that's right for you. He loves you like no earthly father ever will; he wants only good things for you.

9

YOU ARE OF GREAT VALUE

(Nobodies)

Shiri shuffled into the synagogue as she did every Sabbath. She craned her head upward to compensate for her back, which was bowed over. This was the only way she could see what was ahead. The pain that accompanied this maneuver shot down her spine and caused her to grind her teeth, so she could only hold her head up for a few seconds. In those few seconds, Shiri saw the synagogue was packed full and there was no space for her. Word of the young prophet had brought everyone out.

She felt deep disappointment. Because of her difficulty looking ahead, Shiri only ventured out of her home on the Sabbath. For one day a week, she would endure the pain. She enjoyed being with other people; she enjoyed listening to God's Word being read out loud, even if it meant staring at the ground the whole time.

She winced as she forced her head up farther, hoping her first glance was wrong, but there was no space for her. She paused and took a deep breath. She'd so hoped to hear this Jesus speak. If only half of what they said of him were true, he'd be a joy to hear. She sighed and started to shuffle out of the synagogue.

"Take my place," a young woman's voice said.

She paused, then turned, clenching her teeth as she lifted her head to search out where the voice had come from. A hand waved from the back of the synagogue, and Shiri recognized a young woman who lived near her. She shuffled over to the girl, apologizing all the way as she bumped into people. Most just ignored her, but some grumbled at her.

"Thank you, Naomi," she said when she reached the spot. "Are you sure?"

"Yes. I can listen from the door," Naomi said as she stood up.

Shiri dropped to the spot Naomi had vacated and rested her hands against the floor to steady herself. People talked all around her, and she enjoyed catching up on the gossip and news. They talked around her, but no one ever talked to her.

Shiri remembered another time. A time when she was young and pretty like Naomi. A time when she walked upright. A time when the young men vied for her attention. Then it happened. She woke up one morning all bent over, and she'd spent the last eighteen years that way.

The crowd quieted. A calm voice began to speak. Shiri took a deep breath and angled her head up to catch a glimpse of the speaker. So that was Jesus. Shiri had trouble matching the man with the stories.

She expected a tall muscular man who dressed like a prince. Such a man could cast out demons with his word, but not this man. This man just looked like—well, a shepherd. "Is that Jesus?" she whispered to the woman next to her.

"Quiet," the woman said.

He continued to teach, and as Shiri looked at the ground and focused on only his voice, she began to sense a power. This man understood God's Word like no one did and spoke it as if he knew it intimately. The man she saw didn't look like a great prophet, but the man she heard sounded like one.

Stories of Jesus healing people ran all through Judea. He'd healed blind people and lepers, and there were rumors of him raising the dead. Could he heal her? He probably could, except he wouldn't do it today. Not on the Sabbath.

A tear dropped onto the floor. Of all the days to run into a great prophet, it had to be this day. Maybe she should call out to him anyway. What harm could it do?

Shiri banished the thought. The rabbis more than once had told her she'd been afflicted by a devil, that some sin in her life brought this upon her. If she called out in the synagogue, they'd tell Jesus what a sinner she was, and no prophet of God would heal a sinner.

Her arms weakened and Shiri let her face fall to the ground. She was so weary of this affliction. She closed her eyes and wept silently.

An elbow struck her ribcage.

"I'm sorry," Shiri said. "I'll be quiet."

"Didn't you hear him?"

Shiri pushed herself up and turned her head sideways to face the woman. "What?"

"Jesus. He just told you to go up there."

In her tears, Shiri had heard nothing. Her arms began to shake with fear. Had she offended him? Did he know about her sin? What would he do?

She forced herself to her feet and shuffled toward the front of the synagogue. The crowd parted, making a path for her to follow. She didn't want to face this man of God's eyes. She didn't want to see his anger. She stopped before him and stared at his feet.

"Woman, you are set free from your infirmity" (Luke 13:12 NIV).

He put his hands on her. Warmth rushed from his hands through her whole back. For eighteen years Shiri had felt like she carried a boulder, and suddenly that boulder had sprung from her back. She stood up and raised her hands, praising God.

On a Sabbath Jesus was teaching in one of the synagogues, and a woman was there who had been crippled by a spirit for eighteen years. She was bent over and could not straighten up at all. When Jesus saw her, he called her forward and said to her, "Woman, you are set free from your infirmity." Then he put his hands on her, and immediately she straightened up and praised God.

Indignant because Jesus had healed on the Sabbath, the synagogue ruler said to the people, "There are six days for work. So come and be healed on those days, not on the Sabbath."

The Lord answered him, "You hypocrites! Doesn't each of you on the Sabbath untie his ox or donkey from the stall and lead it out to give it water? Then should not this woman, a daughter of Abraham, whom Satan has kept bound for eighteen long years, be set free on the Sabbath day from what bound her?"

When he said this, all his opponents were humiliated, but the people were delighted with all the wonderful things he was doing. (Luke 13:10–17 NIV)

When I read this passage about the woman I've called Shiri, I was intrigued. She just didn't seem to be behaving right. Here she was in Jesus' presence. The Scriptures make it clear "Jesus saw her." She must have heard the stories of healing, yet she didn't even try to lift a finger to get his attention. This is strange behavior for a woman who needs healing.

No one else who needed healing was this shy.

A leper cried out to him to be cleansed (Matt. 8:2).

A centurion sent the Jewish elders to get Jesus to come and heal his servant (Luke 7:1–10).

The paralytic's friends broke into the roof of where he was meeting to get to him (Luke 5:18–25).

The woman with the issue of blood sneaked up behind him to touch his garment (Matt. 9:20).

Two blind men followed him, crying out for mercy (Matt. 9:27–31).

A Canaanite mother who could expect no mercy from a Jewish prophet hunted him down to get a demon cast out of her daughter (Matt. 15:21–28).

And this bent-over woman who suffered for eighteen years sat quietly in the synagogue listening to the sermon. Why? I think because she thought she was nobody. I think she thought she had no right to disturb the meeting; I think she thought herself unworthy of healing.

Think of your own church. Think of those quiet people who sit in the back. Maybe they aren't physically appealing, or maybe they're poor. Just how much attention do they get? How welcome do they feel?

In 1980, Canada suffered through a recession. My

wife and I moved from Vernon to Salmon Arm hoping work prospects would be better there. Thanks to God forcing us to go to the Salvation Army as discussed in the prior chapter, we knew we had to find a church—so we went looking.

In one church we visited, they asked new people to stand up and introduce themselves. So I stood up, gave our names, and quipped I worked for the federal government.

Well, after church was over, key people of the fellowship surrounded us, asking when we moved there, where we lived, and all the usual questions. They wanted to make sure that I, the "government employee" knew I was welcome. The recession was hurting churches, too, so someone with a good-paying government job would be a welcome addition to the fellowship.

Finally, someone asked what I did for the federal government. (If I haven't mentioned it already, I should mention it now. I have a quick wit, and I'm not afraid to use it.)

I told them I worked for the funds-redistribution branch.

"The what?" someone asked.

"The funds-redistribution branch," I repeated. "I collect unemployment insurance from the federal government, and then spend it." I smiled; no one else did.

I think that's when I first really learned the lesson of somebody/nobody. When I first mentioned that I worked for the federal government, I was a somebody. What I said mattered. I was important.

When people found out I was just making fun of receiving government help, I became a nobody. What I said didn't matter. No one really needed to get to know me.

In spite of the snub, it was the best of the churches we visited, and we continued to attend there. And even though we couldn't "contribute" to the church, some people in that fellowship learned of the hardships we'd endured and took us under their wing. There were God-loving people in that church who loved us, even though we couldn't give anything back.

Those people really got behind us when we had a third premature child. They helped us out with prayer, finances, and contacts in Vancouver where the hospital for premature babies was.

We learned that to those who love Jesus, everyone is a somebody.

Another time I really saw the lesson in practice is when we hired a receptionist for the company where I work. We put an ad in the paper. Some resumes came by fax, some by mail, but only one person came to our office.

This visit to the office impressed us, because our office is located in an industrial area and isn't exactly easy to find or get to. This woman took the trouble to dress up, find us, and hand in a resume.

Lucky for her, both the owner and I were there to witness this. We glanced at the resume and hired her for no better reason than she took all that trouble to apply for the job.

Now, this woman was a nobody in the world's eyes. She was and still is a single mother. She was collecting welfare. She was the least of our citizenry. Since I'd been as poor as she was, I had a pretty good idea how society treated her.

It's probably a good thing we just glanced at her resume and asked only a few questions. After we hired her, we found out she couldn't even type!

But she answered the phones well, knew how to file, and seemed to be able to tolerate our unique style of doing business, so we didn't care. She later learned how to type using computer software.

As time progressed, we needed a purchasing agent. By this time, she'd proven herself a quick learner and a competent employee, so we gave her the job—and this is where I chuckle.

When she first came to us, she was a nobody. Then, salesmen who dropped in were polite but paid her no special attention. Now that she's the purchasing agent, the one who decides what we buy and from whom, these same salesmen trip over themselves to be kind to her and make her feel like a somebody.

Those salesmen probably wouldn't have spit on her if she was on fire before she came to work for us. Now they listen attentively to her every word and make sure she has plenty of chocolates at Christmas. And therein lies the problem.

We live in a world where our looks, our wealth, our position, or our power defines our worth. We can go from nobody to somebody and back to nobody so easily.

Right now, I'm a somebody. I'm the controller of one of the larger businesses in my community. Today I'm going for an expensive lunch with the agent of our insurance company—he'll be paying and I can order whatever I want. He'll laugh at my jokes. He'll care what I think. But if I lose this job tomorrow, the next time we have lunch I'll probably pay—if we have lunch at all.

My job makes me somebody—in this world.

My lack of a job makes me nobody—in this world.

My relationship with Christ makes me somebody, in this world and the world to come.

How do I know this? I know this because of Shiri. Jesus said something that struck me.

> Then should not this woman, a daughter of Abraham, whom Satan has kept bound for eighteen long years, be set free on the Sabbath day from what bound her? (Luke 13:16 NIV)

Focus on "should not this woman." Why didn't he say "a woman"? I think he was making a point here. Not long before, Jewish elders were begging him to heal the centurion's servant because the centurion had built them a synagogue. That man was a somebody, but "this woman" was a nobody. I'm speculating that if Jesus had healed someone important, no one would've been complaining about what day he'd done it.

No religious leader in history has treated women

like Jesus did. Women of that era lived in a culture that encouraged their silence, that devalued their worth. So what does he do? He picks a crippled "nobody" of a woman to make whole again. He didn't care what day of the week it was, and he certainly didn't care she was "nobody." He didn't care because Jesus loves all his children, man or woman, nobody or somebody.

Fortunately, women in today's culture are free from many of the social biases of Shiri's day. Or are they?

Not too long ago, I saw a young lady perform on a popular talk show. The whole world has watched this girl grow up because she's been on television since her childhood. I think most people would agree she's attractive and has a wonderful personality, and yet …

Her head looked out of proportion to her body because she had starved herself thin. She didn't always look this way. Why did she do it? She already had looks, money, and talent. Who convinced her that now she has to starve herself? Who made her feel she was a nobody if she didn't lose those pounds?

Women are being bombarded by lies. They might as well be hunched over like Shiri, with the burden of guilt society is heaping on them.

If you're too fat (and you don't have to have too much extra weight to qualify as fat these days) you're a nobody until you starve yourself thin.

If you're not pretty or shapely, you're a nobody until you get the right cosmetics or surgery to fix the "mistakes" God made.

If you're a stay-at-home mom, you're a nobody until you get those kids into day care and get a "career."

If you're a working single mom, you're a nobody until you get a man in your life.

If you're a teen girl and you haven't "put out" for a boy, you're a nobody until you give your virtue to a young man who'll lie to you until you've given him what he wants.

It's time to stop the lies.

If you love the Lord Jesus Christ, you're a somebody no matter what your situation. You don't need makeup or surgery to get Jesus' approval. He doesn't care what size dress you can fit into. He doesn't care if you can sing as long as you make a "joyful noise." All he cares is that you love him because he loves you.

Someone wrote that if you were the only person needing saving, Jesus would have gone to the cross just for you. Don't let anyone tell you you're nobody. How can you possibly be a nobody when the creator of the universe died on a cross to save you? If he loves you, nothing else matters, because to the only one who really does matter—Jesus—you are, and always will be, a somebody.

10

I'LL GET THERE WHEN I GET THERE

(POWER)

The donkey let out a loud bray and fell to its knees. Issachar jumped off and raised a stick to beat the animal to its feet, but paused before delivering the blow. Sweat and foam covered the poor creature's body. He'd driven it to exhaustion searching from village to village in Perea. More beatings would only drive the donkey to its death.

"Find Jesus."

Martha's words echoed in his mind. Those were the only two words their mistress had spoken, but each servant knew exactly what Martha meant. Find Jesus or Lazarus will die. So each servant took a donkey and a direction and set out to find Jesus.

Leaving the donkey to fend for itself, Issachar started to run. He ran because a face in his mind drove him—the anguished face of Martha, the much-beloved woman he served. She spoke only two words, but the tears she shed in fear of losing Lazarus pushed his heart when his body wanted to quit.

For Martha, Issachar ran until his lungs lit on fire. For Martha, he walked only long enough to catch his breath and started to run again. He did this for two hours.

His legs burned and his lungs gasped for air when he stumbled into the next village. The previous village said Jesus had come here. With every fiber of his being, he now sought the same Jesus he went to Jerusalem to betray to the high priest.

Martha had found out about his visit to Jerusalem. Instead of casting him out of her home, she forgave him, because she said that's what Jesus would want her to do. In his heart, Issachar swore his life to Martha's service that day.

Issachar spotted some men loitering near the stable. He half ran, half staggered over to them. He opened his mouth to speak, but his lungs stole great gasps of air rather than letting him talk.

"Friend," a curly haired man said, "what's the matter?"

More gasps before his heart slowed to a canter. "Jesus . . . I need to find Jesus."

The men exchanged glances with one another.

Issachar dropped his arms loosely to his side. "He's not here?"

Curly scratched his scruffy cheek. "He might be."

Issachar straightened as creeping anger started to overcome physical exhaustion. "Might be? What does that mean?"

Curly smiled. "He might be here, but I'm having trouble remembering where." The man's eyes drifted to Issachar's money purse.

Issachar bit his tongue to keep harsh words from escaping. "How much?" he said through gritted teeth.

"Well, friend," Curly said, "*you* don't look sick, but the way you stumbled into town, I'd say you really love the person who *is* sick. I think you love that person enough to hand over the whole purse."

"Forget it," Issachar said. "I'll find him myself."

The men formed a circle around him.

"It may not be that easy to find him," Curly said.

Anger now completely overtook exhaustion. Issachar had no idea where the strength came from, but it came. He clenched his hands into fists. These men spent their days loitering about; he spent many of his days working hard in the fields. It would be easy to strike these men down, to batter them into submission. Imagine extorting money from those who needed to see Jesus. He took a deep breath before striking, then stopped.

Hadn't he gone to the high priest to betray Jesus, to betray Martha, for money? Issachar looked into the faces of each of the men and realized he was looking into his own face. He pulled his money purse free from his belt and tossed it to Curly.

"Wise decision," Curly said. "Just keep heading down the main road to the square. If he isn't there now, he'll eventually show up there."

Issachar glared into Curly's eyes as he stepped toward the man and drove his shoulder into his chest, knocking him backward. "Thanks," he said, and ran for the square.

Through blurred eyes, he saw a crowd in the square. His heart managed to leap with hope while at the same time pounding from exhaustion.

A crowd had to mean Jesus. The Jesus who loved Martha and Lazraus. He staggered to a stop at the edge of the crowd and then pushed his way through to the center, ignoring the complaints of those he displaced.

He broke through the inner ring and stood face-to-face with Jesus. Jesus stopped talking and looked directly at Issachar. Suddenly, he felt naked. This man knew; he knew Issachar had betrayed him to the high priest. A deep sense of dread overtook him. Issachar started to turn so he could run from the face of this … man?

"Find Jesus."

Martha's words. Find Jesus or Lazarus will die.

For Martha he steeled himself and turned to Jesus. "Lord, the one you love is sick."

Now a man named Lazarus was sick. He was from Bethany, the village of Mary and her sister Martha. This Mary, whose brother Lazarus now lay sick, was the same one who poured perfume on the Lord and wiped his feet with her hair. So the sisters sent word to Jesus, "Lord, the one you love is sick."

When he heard this, Jesus said, "This sickness will not end in death. No, it is for God's glory so that God's Son may be glorified through it." Jesus loved Martha and her sister and Lazarus. Yet when he heard that Lazarus was sick, he stayed where he was two more days.

Then he said to his disciples, "Let us go back to Judea."

"But Rabbi," they said, "a short while ago the Jews tried to stone you, and yet you are going back there?"

Jesus answered, "Are there not twelve hours of daylight? A man who walks by day will not stumble, for he sees by this world's light. It is when he walks by night that he stumbles, for he has no light."

After he had said this, he went on to tell them, "Our friend Lazarus has fallen asleep; but I am going there to wake him up."

His disciples replied, "Lord, if he sleeps, he will get better." Jesus had been speaking of his death, but his disciples thought he meant natural sleep.

So then he told them plainly, "Lazarus is dead, and for your sake I am glad I was not there, so that you may believe. But let us go to him."

Then Thomas (called Didymus) said to the rest of the disciples, "Let us also go, that we may die with him." (John 11:1–16 NIV)

People spoke around her and to her, but Martha didn't hear them. She was awake, but everything around her felt like a dream. Any moment she would wake up and go to find Lazarus asleep in his room. She'd wake him and Mary, and the three of them would enjoy a meal before starting the day. But it was only a dream, because Jesus hadn't come.

When Issachar told Martha and Mary what Jesus had said, Martha thought he was lying. She thought he hadn't gone at all and just sold the donkey and spent the money. But then why would he come back, why would he be physically exhausted from a hard journey? It crushed her to think that the Jesus she'd given shelter to, that she'd given her faith to, didn't come and heal her brother. Lazarus was Jesus' friend, and Jesus had let him die.

Jesus had healed so many. Many of them were worthy of his healing, but many were not. He'd forgiven the unforgivable and healed the unworthy because they had faith. Martha had faith. She had believed, and yet he hadn't come. She buried her face in her hands and wept.

A hand rested on her shoulder. Martha looked up to see Issachar. Beads of sweat ran down his face, and he heaved from shortness of breath.

"I saw him," he gasped.

Martha took a deep breath and put a temporary dam on her tears. "Saw who?"

"Jesus. I was out in the field and I saw Jesus. He's coming here."

"Here?"

Issachar nodded.

Martha jumped to her feet and rushed to Mary's room. Her sister lay facedown on her bed.

"He's coming."

Mary rolled over and wiped her red eyes with her sleeve.

"Who's coming?"

"Jesus."

Mary stared at her as if she didn't understand.

"Jesus is coming. Issachar saw him from the fields."

Mary rolled facedown back on the bed. Martha rushed to Mary's side and shook her sister's shoulder. "We have to go meet him."

Mary turned to her side and looked at her. "Why? Lazarus is dead. Nothing can be done."

"I can't believe that," Martha said. "I just can't."

Martha pushed past her questioning friends and bolted out the doorway. She ran as fast as a woman her age could run. Everything around her stayed a blur except the road ahead. Somewhere on that road she'd find him, and somehow she just knew he could make it right.

Martha rounded a bend in the road and came face-to-face with Jesus and those who traveled with him. She fell to her knees before him. Jesus motioned for her to stand up. Martha rose and asked him the question that had tormented her.

On his arrival, Jesus found that Lazarus had already been in the tomb for four days. Bethany was less than two miles from Jerusalem, and many Jews had come to Martha and Mary to comfort them in the loss of their brother. When Martha heard that Jesus was coming, she went out to meet him, but Mary stayed at home.

"Lord," Martha said to Jesus, "if you had been here, my brother would not have died. But I know that even now God will give you whatever you ask."

Jesus said to her, "Your brother will rise again."

Martha answered, "I know he will rise again in the resurrection at the last day."

Jesus said to her, "I am the resurrection and the life. He who believes in me will live, even though he dies; and whoever lives and believes in me will never die. Do you believe this?"

"Yes, Lord," she told him, "I believe that you are the Christ, the Son of God, who was to come into the world." (John 11:17–27 NIV)

Mary smiled politely at the condolences one of the neighbor women offered. The thought of Jesus' coming stole any hope of hiding in her bed. She had to get ready for his arrival.

Martha burst into the room, her eyes searching until they fell on Mary. Her sister rushed over to her. Martha's breath came in short gasps; she'd been running.

"The Teacher is here," she said, "and is asking for you."

Mary looked into Martha's eyes and saw something she hadn't seen for days. Hope. Could it be?

She bolted out the door, only barely aware that the house had emptied behind her and everyone was following her. Mary ran like the wind, her heart pounding more from longing than exhaustion. She'd cried until she thought she could cry no more, then cried again. She thought her soul had died, but when she heard Jesus had asked for her, it stirred, it drove her to him.

She rounded the bend in the road, and there stood Jesus. Mary's legs weakened; she fell at his feet. Despair overwhelmed her; her tears flowed. In a broken voice, she said, "Lord, if you had been here, my brother would not have died."

Jesus looked down at her, then at the crowd that followed her. Mary realized many of them were weeping too. Suddenly Jesus looked old and weighed down.

"Where have you laid him?" he asked.

Before she had a chance to answer, someone in the crowd spoke.

"Come and see, Lord."

Mary stopped breathing. The crowd went deathly silent. Jesus was weeping.

Someone broke the silence.

"See how he loved him!"

Yes, Mary thought, *Jesus loved Lazarus. Why hadn't he come? Why did he let it happen?*

Someone spoke her thoughts out loud.

"Could not he who opened the eyes of the blind man have kept this man from dying?"

Jesus ignored the comment. He started to follow the one who said, "Come and see, Lord."

Mary watched as he moved away. What was he going to do? She scrambled to her feet and followed. (Dialogue based on John 11:28–37 NIV.)

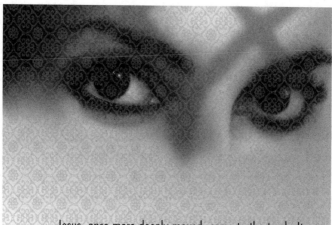

Jesus, once more deeply moved, came to the tomb. It was a cave with a stone laid across the entrance. "Take away the stone," he said.

"But, Lord," said Martha, the sister of the dead man, "by this time there is a bad odor, for he has been there four days."

Then Jesus said, "Did I not tell you that if you believed, you would see the glory of God?"

So they took away the stone. Then Jesus looked up and said, "Father, I thank you that you have heard me. I knew that you always hear me, but I said this for the benefit of the people standing here, that they may believe that you sent me."

When he had said this, Jesus called in a loud voice, "Lazarus, come out!" The dead man came out, his hands and feet wrapped with strips of linen, and a cloth around his face.

Jesus said to them, "Take off the grave clothes and let him go." (John 11:38–44 NIV)

Jesus meant to send a message the day he raised Lazarus from the dead. The message may have made a small popping noise in a backward country in a nowhere part of the Roman Empire, but it has since rocked history.

Jesus had already raised people from the dead, but they'd been dead for only a short while. I can almost see Jesus rubbing his chin and thinking to himself: "I'll bet some scholar is going to say when I raised those people from the dead I simply performed CPR. They'll say it was no miracle at all. They'll say I was just a paramedic ahead of his time."

Well, Mr. Scholar—explain Lazarus. What man in his right mind would spend four days holed up in a tomb wrapped in strips of linen just to pull off a publicity stunt for his buddy Jesus? Imagine spending four days in complete and utter darkness with no food or water.

No one in their right mind would endure four days of solitude, along with thirst and starvation, just to pull the wool over everyone's eyes. Lazarus was as dead as dead can be.

So on the day that Jesus stood in front of the tomb, he sent a message to all humanity, both present and future: I have power, and my power is unlimited. I can drag back a soul that has since left this world; I can rebuild a body that has already started to decompose— all with just three spoken words: "Lazarus, come out!" Top that!

We humans run to power like moths to a light bulb. We can't help but be impressed by it, seduced by it. If we know someone with power, we want everyone else to know we know that person.

But just how great is earthly power?

Some have what seems like unlimited power. The president of the United States has been called the most powerful man in the free world. The queen of England can still pardon criminals, even though she's considered a "figurehead." Some would say the presidents of certain corporations have more power than either of them.

But the interesting thing about power in this world is how limited it really is. The people who put him there can remove the president of the United States from power. And his power is limited in what it can do. He can order the military to war, but he can't make a blind man see. He can raise or lower taxes, but only with the approval of Congress.

Imagine someone who lived their whole life knowing every president who occupied the White House. Imagine if that someone had the ear of every president. What good would it do him on his deathbed during that split second when he passed from this world to the next?

Imagine standing before God on judgment day and using as your best defense letters of recommendation from all the presidents who lived during your lifetime. God would ask only one question—did you know the one who had real power?

Jesus had real power because it couldn't be limited. No one could walk up to him and say, "You can't do that" or "That can't be done." If Jesus spoke, it happened.

Earthly power is fleeting at best and hardly worth the effort of pursuing.

When I tried to get my first novel published, I kept running up against brick walls. Publishers get thousands of manuscripts every year and only publish less than 1 percent of the submissions they receive.

Through a writer's group, I learned that the road to publication was to make myself stand out. I had to go to a writer's conference where book and magazine editors were available to meet with writers. If you impressed them, you had a good chance of getting your manuscript fast-tracked on the road to publication.

What really struck me at these conferences is how much celebrity status these editors enjoyed. They had special-colored name tags that let you know they were editors. I found myself looking at the name tag before I even looked at the face of the person wearing it. These were the people to meet. These were the people you wanted to sit next to at dinner.

In that small world of "writer's conference," these people had the power. If you impressed them, they had the power to get your book into publication. For that reason, people listened to every word they said. Every joke they made got a laugh. If they said something I didn't agree with, I kept silent. If they said something I did agree with, I made sure they knew it.

During one quiet moment in my room, I remember asking myself, "What's going on here?"

You see, in my world outside the writer's conference I had the power. My students at my part-time teaching position at the college had to listen to me. My clients had to listen to me if they didn't want problems with their bank or the government. In my world I was a professional—a somebody with some power.

At the conference, I was just another writer who believed he had the best book in the world, trying to curry favor with a book editor—a book editor who for those three days had the power.

I have to say, though, that the conferences I've gone to have been for Christian writers, and I've never met an editor yet who let it go to his or her head. I found them to be gracious and tireless in listening to each writer's pitch, and gentle when they had to tell someone they had a long way to go before they'd have something publishable.

But you know, after the conference ended I went back to my world and the editors went back to theirs. They went back to the world where professional accountants are higher on society's food chain than book editors are. After the three days were over, their power was gone.

I've always wanted to ask book editors if they get depressed after the conference. For three days they matter, then when they get home and suddenly they go from celebrity to just the gal or guy who works at some publishing place.

My father, who was a plumber, says the most important person in the palace is the plumber when the toilet is plugged.

If we chase worldly power, we might as well get the doctor to write us a prescription for depression right now. That power is a phantom. Worldly power has limits;

it only matters in certain places, and it disappears ever so easily.

But not so with Jesus' power. He has unlimited power that will last for eternity. The amazing thing is Jesus uses his power for us. There are no Bible stories of Jesus' using his power for himself. He didn't feed himself during the forty days in the wilderness, but he did feed the five thousand.

He must've gotten blisters from his long walks. There's no record of his healing his own feet, but he made the lame walk again.

Satan tempted Jesus sorely, but Jesus didn't strike back. When Satan's demons possessed a poor girl, Jesus used his power to send them all packing.

Brutal men prepared to stone a woman caught in adultery, and he used his power to spare her life—but when they flogged him, Jesus didn't stop it. All he had to do was utter three words—"kill them all"—and the angels would've turned the planet into a nuclear wasteland—but he didn't.

Jesus' incredible, unlimited power is being spent on us—his children. When the powerful step on you, just remember—they stepped on Jesus, too. But also remember that the one with real power will never step on you. He loves you and will return for you someday. You might be "just a janitor" in this world, but you are the child of the King in the next world. As for those who are powerful here, pray for them—because in the next world they will be most miserable if they don't find Jesus.

When I was in junior high school, I had some trouble with a few other students. I'd become sort of a project of theirs—a project of torment. For some reason (to this day I don't know why), one of the older students took me under his wing. He made it perfectly clear: mess with Andy, you mess with me. You didn't want to mess with this guy.

I enjoyed that year. I enjoyed being under the wing of a guy with power. School would have continued to be great if that fellow hadn't gone and graduated. The next year, he was gone. I had to fight my own battles. The power I had reveled in was no more.

I don't ever have to worry about Jesus doing that. Jesus—with unlimited power, unlimited love, and unlimited grace—isn't going anywhere.

11

UNEXPECTED ALLY

(Courage)

Pontius Pilate's wife, Claudia, opened her mouth to call her
maids to dress her. There was commotion all over the city, and she
just had to know what was going on.

Once she was suitably attired to leave the bedchamber, she'd
have an escort take her to the praetorium. Before she could utter any
words, the room around her vanished. The stone floor became an

earthen floor. People were weeping and wailing. Claudia moved through them as though she wasn't even there.

She found the source of the grief. A beautiful young girl lay still. Claudia reached to stroke the child's soft, dark hair, but her fingers passed right through. Claudia jumped back. Did this mean that Claudia had died? Was she going to have to walk in the shadow world?

A commotion started behind her. Claudia turned, and four men had entered. The people in the room seemed to defer to him.

He spoke. "Do not weep; she is not dead, but sleeping."

They laughed at him; they scorned him. Claudia marveled at how quickly they turned on him.

The man moved through the people and stood by the girl. He took the child's delicate hand in his own. His hand was powerful and rough. This man was familiar with hard work. He said, "Little girl, arise."

Claudia sucked in a short breath when the girl sat right up and started chattering and asking for food. The crowd's laughter dropped like a deer hit by a hunter's arrow. (Dialogue and events based on Luke 8:51–55.)

Suddenly, the room lost its shape. It waved like the heat rising off the hot desert floor and disappeared entirely. She could make out shapes off in the distance. Roman soldiers were wrapping a scarlet robe around the man who healed the little girl. They bowed down to the man and mocked him. Why would they do this to him?

Next, the soldiers faded, and Claudia found herself in a barren place. The man was resting, surrounded by his men. She heard what sounded like a flock of geese approaching. She turned, and a multitude of people approached—thousands of people chattering.

Claudia quickly moved to where the man stood. The crowd stopped before him, then went silent. They were waiting for him to speak.

She could tell the man was weary, but still he got to his feet and then started to speak to the crowd. He told them about a kingdom, God's kingdom. This confused Claudia. He talked as if there were only one God.

She found herself mesmerized by his speech. Everything he said she knew to be true. If this man's words ever got back to Pilate, he'd kill him. Pilate would have no choice. Caesar claimed to be God. Pilate couldn't allow anyone to put himself above Caesar if he were to keep his position.

Claudia's mouth dropped open. He stopped speaking, then started through the crowd. He touched people who suffered with illness. Before her very eyes Claudia saw people healed. Who could possibly have this kind of power — unless this man was from God. Was he God?

The sun was getting low in the sky. People were looking tired and hungry. His men spoke to him, told him to send the people away. The man seemed unconcerned. He ordered the crowd to sit down in groups. He held up some bread and fish and blessed it. Claudia was stunned as she watched this small amount of provision passed through the crowd.

The crowd ate. The crowd ate well, and there were baskets of food left over. Was there any limit to this man's power? (Events take from Luke 9:10–17.)

Without warning, Claudia found herself in a garden. It was night and the air was pleasant. Men lay about slumbering. The man approached and stood for a moment looking at the men. He looked like a father watching his children, then he spoke: "Are you still sleeping and resting? Behold, the hour is at hand, and the Son of Man is being betrayed into the hands of sinners. Rise, let us be going. See, my betrayer is at hand."

The men stirred and stood up as a crowd entered the garden.

They had swords and clubs, but they weren't Romans. They had to be temple guards.

One man stepped forward from the guards. He tentatively approached the man and spoke before kissing him.

The guards rushed forward and grabbed the man. One of his own men drew a sword and swung it wildly. A servant fell, clutching the side of his face.

The man spoke. "Put your sword in its place, for all who take the sword will perish by the sword. Or do you think that I cannot now pray to my Father, and He will provide me with more than twelve legions of angels? How then could the Scriptures be fulfilled, that it must happen thus?" (Dialogue and events taken from Matt. 26:45–54.)

The scene in front of her blurred. Suddenly, Roman soldiers moved through the crowd, but it was as if the people didn't even notice them. Claudia recognized the centurion. He served her husband. These soldiers were under Pilate's command.

They forced the scarlet robe around him again. Claudia sank to her knees when they took thorns and wove them in the shape of a crown. They pushed the crown down onto his head, and the thorns cut into his scalp and forehead. Rivulets of blood streamed down his cheeks.

Claudia waited. She waited for the man to use his powers to kill the soldiers, but instead he said nothing. He seemed resigned to a fate that only he understood. Claudia wept as they mocked and spat on him. She winced as they struck him about the head with a reed.

It all faded. Now she stood on a hill where the women near her were wailing. She looked where the women looked. That kind and just man hung from a cross. Claudia fell to the ground and wailed too.

Was this to be her fate? To spend eternity in the shadowlands watching this man's cruel fate? She howled and cried out to him to release her from this eternal sentence of horror.

Claudia awoke on her knees in her bedchamber. She could hear what sounded like a riot outside. She rushed to the doorway to the next room where her maids waited. "What's happening?"

"Pilate is trying that Jewish preacher Jesus of Nazareth," one of the maids said.

Claudia put her hand to her mouth. "No, he can't."

The maids all looked at her in surprise; they couldn't understand why she would care. She knew what they thought. Pilate tried and executed people all the time, and Claudia never spoke against it. Why now?

Why now? Because Claudia knew who this man was. He could call down twelve legions of angels if he wanted. The whole might of the Roman army would be like an ant crushed by this man's heel if he chose. But that wasn't the real reason Claudia cared. Claudia cared because she knew this man. This was a good man, a righteous man; he didn't deserve to die.

"Dress me," she said.

The maids hesitated.

"Dress me!"

They jumped to their feet and quickly dressed Claudia in a manner befitting the governor's wife. "Call for an escort," she said.

One of the maids disappeared and returned with four of Pilate's personal guards. Pilate wouldn't let any of the regular soldiers guard her. He said they were really only slaves who would just as easily kill him as fight for him.

Claudia looked at the battle-hardened men. They sported scars on their muscular arms and faces. They looked none too happy to be there. She'd pulled them away from the fun, and they probably thought she just wanted to go for a walk.

Suddenly, she didn't feel so sure about her conviction to inter-cede for this man. Pilate didn't like it when his decisions were questioned. He was a decent husband as far as Romans went, but he was also governor in the middle of a trial. How would he take her interfering? It wasn't unheard of for a governor to send his wife into exile if she forgot her place.

"What do you wish?" a gruff voice said.

Claudia's mouth went dry. The dreams slammed through her con-sciousness; Claudia had no choice. She stammered out the words. "I wish to see the governor."

The soldiers exchanged glances. The biggest of them shook his head. "That's not possible. He's dealing with the Jews right now. He won't be disturbed."

Claudia thought of the man in the dream. She knew he was this Jesus whom Pilate was trying. She knew he was the one who knew about God, who had the power to raise the dead, to feed the hungry, to bring truth. She took a deep breath and squared her shoulders.

"He will be disturbed by me. I have something important to tell him, and if I tell him when it's too late, you will explain to him why."

Fear flashed across the soldier's eyes. He snapped to attention and spun on his heels. Claudia followed them as they marched to the judgment seat. They stopped short of stepping out into the open. Instead, they parted to let her pass.

Claudia felt unsure until she saw the man, until she saw Jesus. There he stood, making no attempt to argue for himself. He seemed resigned to what was going to happen. She would have to cross in front of everyone and interrupt Pilate while he argued with the Jewish leaders. This just wasn't done.

"Claudia," a familiar voice said behind her. "You shouldn't be here."

Claudia turned and saw Justinius, a centurion of Pilate's guard.

His wife had been a good friend to her, helping her to adapt to life in this backward country.

"I have to speak to Pilate. I have to warn him."

Justinius stiffened and his hand went to the hilt of his sword. "Warn him about what? Is he in danger?"

"Yes," Claudia said.

Justinius turned to the soldiers. "Bring out the reserves."

"Wait," Claudia said. "He's not in that kind of danger."

"Then what kind of danger?"

Claudia indicated Justinius should follow her out of earshot of the soldiers. There she told him the dream.

His looked into her eyes. "You believe this dream came from the gods?"

Claudia shook her head. "No, I believe this dream came from the God. The God with the power to destroy us all."

Justinius chewed on his lower lip. "I will go to Pilate. What is your message?"

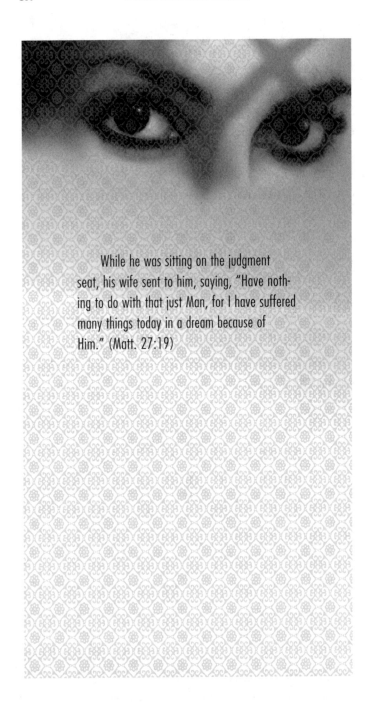

While he was sitting on the judgment seat, his wife sent to him, saying, "Have nothing to do with that just Man, for I have suffered many things today in a dream because of Him." (Matt. 27:19)

You might be saying right now, "Wait a minute. This book is called *When God Met a Girl*. Pilate's wife never met Jesus."

Physically, no. Claudia Procola—which, by the way, is believed to be her true name—probably never met Jesus face-to-face, but she met him nonetheless. She had some kind of dream that was so powerful it convinced her that Jesus was a "just Man." It was so powerful it compelled her to interrupt Pontius Pilate while he sat on the judgment seat.

Interrupting Pilate on the judgment seat might sound like no biggie. She was his wife, after all. Here's an excerpt from a sermon by Pastor Nicholas Brie.

> Claudia most certainly was taking a big chance. That is, Pilate was a violent man. He is well known in history for being brutal, for putting to death many people for the least sign of rebelliousness. Pilate most certainly was abusive to Claudia, especially if she went against him in some way. So here, sending a message to him while he is in the public eye telling him what to do had to have enraged him against her.[1]

Claudia Procola was a woman of great courage. She risked her life for a man she'd never actually met. She risked her life to do the right thing.

Courage manifests in many forms. I come from a family with a history of courage. My grandfather and my uncle both fought in World War II. My father was a professional boxer who never shied away from trouble in the ring—or out, for that matter. My older brother is an ironworker and earns his living walking on high steel. He also doesn't shy away from trouble.

And then there's me.

I have what's called reluctant courage. If I do the right thing, I do so reluctantly.

When I was a teenager, my mother suggested I take typing instead of shop classes. I think she realized I wasn't like my father or my older brother; I wasn't a tools-and-steel kind of guy. She told me, "I think those computers might be big someday. You should take up typing instead." Who knew?

So, I ended up in a class with twenty teenage girls and one other guy. Mom was a lot smarter than I realized. Not only did I learn a useful skill, but also I got to spend an hour every day in the company of twenty young women.

You'd think there's no way a guy could get into trouble in a typing class. What's the worst that could happen?

The other guy could happen. I'll call him Jake (not his real name). I have no idea why Jake was in that class except that he spent most of his time being a jerk. Whenever the teacher stepped out of the class, he'd hassle one poor girl who suffered from a mental handicap.

Some of the other girls would tell Jake to knock it off, but he just ignored them. For some reason, it made him feel good to taunt this girl.

One day when the teacher had stepped out of the class, this girl managed to type a complete page without any errors. She started to giggle and clap at her accomplishment. She was really just an eight-year-old in a fifteen-year-old's body.

Jake got up from his desk, took a look at the sheet of paper, yanked it from the typewriter, and tore it in half.

Now, you need to understand that Jake was tough. He had a bad reputation, and he dressed the part too. He wore torn blue jeans, black boots, a jean vest, and had greasy hair. I think he even wore a chain bracelet.

My mouth acted long before my more reasonable processes had a chance to have some input. I called him a bad name. He laughed. Throwing common sense out the door, I then suggested he and I step outside.

The exit to the side of the school was just outside the classroom door. Jake and I went out, followed by twenty of the fairer sex. My stomach was churning, and I had to force my hands not to shake. This guy was going to kill me.

We squared off. I hit my best karate stance and said, "Let's go."

I wasn't a Christian back then, but if I had been, I'd swear some angel must have been standing behind me, because this guy's eyes widened and he backed away. "I'm not fighting you," he said. "You know karate."

I did my best not to betray the truth. Everything I learned about karate I learned from the movies. It was all bluster and bluff—and it worked.

Like I said, I have reluctant courage. In spite of my special-forces training, I believe the best form of self-defense is to be able to outrun your opponent.

Oh, I didn't tell you about my special-forces training?

Remember in a previous chapter when I told you about my time in the army cadets? I was later attached to a special unit. We received training that few in the armed forces ever receive. We were a unique unit designed for a special purpose.

Impressed yet? Do you have visions of a muscle-bound, silent killer? Visions of the kind of guy they send into the jungle to rescue all the hostages, and while he's there, he manages to take out a company of the enemy? If you do, you've got the wrong vision.

I was a member of the bagpipe band. We were a special force all right. We were a group of musicians who spent our days in the barracks playing music until someone needed us to march for the tourists. Sorry if I misled you.

The few times I've had to display courage are nothing compared to what Claudia did. Claudia had to interrupt the most powerful man in the country to tell him about a dream. Claudia could have been facing death, but she went to Pilate anyway. She went because she knew who she went for.

Believe it or not, today Jesus asks us to be like Claudia. He has asked us to spread his gospel throughout the world. He asks us to have the courage to tell people about him; even people who don't want to hear about him.

Christians have been killed for spreading Jesus' gospel. In North America, the law protects us from persecution for religious conviction, but in many parts of the world Christians speak of the "just Man" to their own peril. In some places, imprisonment for speaking out about Jesus is not uncommon.

But we have to be courageous, even if it's done with reluctance. Jesus stood before the religious establishment and told them to their faces they were wrong. He stood before the Roman governor and told him he had no power other than what God gave him. He hung on the cross, enduring excruciating pain, just to save us. He had the courage to do what had to be done.

But you know what's really great? We don't have to "pull ourselves up by our bootstraps" to get courage. We just have to ask for it.

It's normal to be afraid. Fear is what keeps us alive. But when you know you need to tell someone about Jesus, when your mouth goes dry, when your knees shake, when your heart starts to speed up, pause for a moment. Whisper a short prayer. Ask Jesus to give you the courage he gave to Claudia. Ask him to give you the courage to speak the truth, to let the world know that Jesus Christ is Lord.

12

EVERYTHING HAS CHANGED

(LOYALTY)

Mary Magdalene jerked in spasms. *Whoosh, crack,* and then her back arched in pain. Chunks of bone ripped into her back, tearing away pieces of flesh. After three lashes, she dropped to her knees and trembled at the thought of another blow. The whip hit, and she howled in agony.

She was covered in sweat when her eyes snapped open. Utter darkness shrouded the room, but Mary's eyes darted about looking for some unseen tormenter. Her chest heaved in short breaths while her heart pounded.

A cold dread fell on her soul. Mary hadn't felt anything like this since the voices lived in her mind. They were in the room. They had to be.

She pulled the bed coverings over her face and huddled into a ball. The feeling of dread worsened. He had sent them away; they couldn't be back. She couldn't hear the voices, but Mary knew they were nearby. A jolt shot through her body as a thought flashed through her mind. They'd done something to him!

Mary threw the coverings off and leapt out of bed. As she felt through the dark for the doorway, her skin prickled with a cold sensation. She found the door and moved quickly through the house, not caring whether her movements woke anyone else or not.

Once outside, Mary ran as if a ravenous wolf was on her heels. She ran to make sure he was okay. She shook her head. He was dead. Only his body remained. So why then did she feel such panic that something had happened to him?

Mary pushed on, despite the fire in her legs, even though sharp pains knifed her ribs.

"Behold, I am bringing him out to you, that you may know that I find no fault in him."

Pilate had found no fault in him. When the governor spoke those words, hope had sprung in Mary's heart. Pilate had found Jesus innocent. They were going to let him go!

Tears stung her eyes as she remembered. The Roman soldiers led her master out. They'd jammed a crown of thorns onto his head. Dried blood caked his hair and face. He wore a purple robe, but it couldn't hide the dark bloodstains. They'd scourged him.

Suddenly, sorrow overwhelmed her. Mary's legs gave out and she half staggered, half walked.

"Behold the man!" Pilate said. Pilate didn't know Jesus. Jesus was more than a man.

Mary's body convulsed.

"Crucify him, crucify him!" That's what the crowd cried out. Crucify him, even though Pilate found him innocent. Crucify Jesus, who'd only told them the truth. Crucify Jesus, who'd healed their sick.

Mary leaned against a wall and panted. Why did they do it?

She started to sob. Pilate had gone back into the praetorium with Jesus. Again, Mary had dared to hope Pilate would ignore the calls of the crowd and let Jesus go. But then he brought Jesus out again.

"Behold your king!" Pilate cried out to the crowd.

Why had he said that? It would only anger the crowd — and it did.

"Away with him, away with him! Crucify him!" the crowd cried out.

Pilate taunted them. "Shall I crucify your king?"

The chief priest answered for the crowd. "We have no king but Caesar!"

Mary slumped to the cold stones. That was it. Pilate gave Jesus over to be crucified. Why?

Jesus was anything but just a man. She remembered how he took authority over the demons that had tormented her. With just words he had ripped their chains from her. With just words she had seen him raise dead people, heal sick people. With just words she had seen him give hope to the people. And in return they killed him.

Mary struggled to her feet and shuffled toward the tomb where he was buried. Brokenhearted, she wanted only to be near him wherever he was.

She shuffled like Jesus did when he bore the cross on his back. They'd scourged him, beaten him, and then forced him to carry the instrument of his own death. He shuffled from the pain and exhaustion of his wounds; Mary shuffled from a broken spirit.

Mary remembered wailing along with the other women. Wailing that the one who'd done so much good was about to be murdered, that the man who'd loved them, who'd given them life and hope, would soon be ripped from the world.

The crowd took great pleasure in taunting him as he moved through the street. Just a week before they'd been singing hosanna — now they laughed and mocked. How could they change so quickly?

She stopped. The tomb wasn't far off. It was still dark. It was dark that day, too. For some reason that day the sky had darkened, as if God himself could no longer watch what was happening.

"Woman, behold your son!" He'd spoken to his mother from the cross. In that intense pain, he took time to tell his mother who was to care for her.

"Behold your mother!" he'd told John. John was to care for Jesus' mother.

Jesus hadn't spoken to her, but Mary Magdalene knew he'd seen her. He'd seen her pain and tears; and even in his own agony, Mary knew he cared about her pain.

"I thirst!" he'd said.

Things became strangely quiet after he said that. Someone raised a sponge of sour wine on hyssop to his mouth, and then he said the words that ripped her heart apart.

"It is finished!"

His head fell to his chest. Their hope was gone.

Mary came to the tomb, and her hand went to her mouth. The stone was gone.

She looked about but saw no one. She started toward the tomb to look inside, then she stopped. Mary knew if she looked in that tomb and his body was gone, she'd never be able to stand the shock.

She turned to leave and then stopped again. She had to know.

Mary edged toward the tomb, just close enough to see inside. She sucked in a deep breath and put her hand to her chest. Why? How?

She turned and ran to where Peter and John were staying. She banged on the door with both fists until it creaked open. Peter stood there. He had the face of a man who would forever be tortured. John stood behind him; he looked worse than Peter.

In short breaths she told them, "They have taken away the Lord out of the tomb, and we do not know where they have laid him."

He looked like he didn't quite understand—then suddenly his eyes widened. Peter pushed past her and ran in the direction of the tomb. John took off after him and gained ground on Peter quickly.

Mary was exhausted. She couldn't run anymore, so she followed them as best as she could at a quick walk. She had no idea why she was even going. They'd stolen his body. What would they do to it? Would they hang it by the gates? Could they hurt him any more than they already had?

Until Jesus, her life had been pointless. The lives of all the women she knew had been pointless. No one cared about them; no one loved them—until Jesus. He had been the first man who treated the women as if they mattered. He had taught them just as he taught the men. He wanted the women to know about God, about the kingdom that would be coming.

Mary stopped for a second and looked to the sky. Jesus said something about his kingdom not being of this world. Did that mean his kingdom was somewhere else? Was his kingdom up there? Is that where he'd gone?

When Mary arrived at the tomb, Peter and John weren't there. Where had they gone? Did they know what happened?

With the dawn light, Mary felt just a little braver. She crept up on the tomb and looked inside. She jumped back and let out a little yelp of surprise. Her legs trembled, and it was all she could do not to faint or turn and run.

Two creatures of unearthly beauty, shimmering in white, were in the tomb. One sat where Jesus' head had lain, the other at the feet.

They spoke at the same time. Their voices sounded like the echoes over water.

"Woman, why are you weeping?"

Why was she weeping? Where had these two been? Didn't they know who'd been in the tomb? Didn't they know what had happened? She was weeping because the only man who had ever loved her purely had rested there.

She answered, "Because they have taken away my Lord, and I do not know where they have laid him."

Mary heard a sound behind her. She spun around; a man stood behind her.

He asked, "Woman, why are you weeping? Whom are you seeking?"

Hope leapt in Mary's chest. This man was probably the gardener. He might have had something to do with what happened to Jesus.

Mary took a few deep breaths and wiped the tears on her face with her sleeve. "Sir, if you have carried him away, tell me where you have laid him, and I will take him away."

He just looked at her, and her hope began to fade. Mary turned back and looked at the empty tomb. Jesus was dead. His body was gone. She hadn't been this completely crushed since the voices lived in her head. They'd ruled over her, stifling her every thought. Now despair ruled over her.

"Mary!"

The air felt and smelled like it did after a lightning storm. Every fiber of her being trembled with anticipation, with hope. Mary turned and just froze. It was Jesus.

"Rabboni!"

All strength left Mary's body. She bowed before him and grabbed his ankles. How could this be? Mary didn't care. Jesus was alive!

He spoke to her: "Do not cling to me, for I have not yet ascended to my Father; but go to my brethren and say to them, 'I am ascending to my Father and your Father, and to my God and your God.'"

Mary reluctantly released him. All she wanted to do was sit in his presence forever, follow him wherever he went. But he'd just given her a command; she had to go tell Peter, John, and the rest of them that Jesus was alive. (Dialogue is based on John 19 and 20:1–18.)

Then the disciples went away again to their own homes. But Mary stood outside by the tomb weeping, and as she wept she stooped down and looked into the tomb. And she saw two angels in white sitting, one at the head and the other at the feet, where the body of Jesus had lain. Then they said to her, "Woman, why are you weeping?"

She said to them, "Because they have taken away my Lord, and I do not know where they have laid Him."

Now when she had said this, she turned around and saw Jesus standing there, and did not know that it was Jesus. Jesus said to her, "Woman, why are you weeping? Whom are you seeking?"

She, supposing Him to be the gardener, said to Him, "Sir, if You have carried Him away, tell me where You have laid Him, and I will take Him away."

Jesus said to her, "Mary!"

She turned and said to Him, "Rabboni!" (which is to say, Teacher).

Jesus said to her, "Do not cling to Me, for I have not yet ascended to My Father; but go to My brethren and say to them, 'I am ascending to My Father and your Father, and to My God and your God.'"

Mary Magdalene came and told the disciples that she had seen the Lord, and that He had spoken these things to her. (John 20:10–18)

Loyalty. Someone who is loyal sticks with you no matter what. Loyal people are those who are still around when you've been kicked into the ditch, and they extend their hands to help you out again. Your relationship with loyal people is based on more than just how each of you can benefit from the relationship.

Mary Magdalene was probably one of the most loyal people in the Bible. She was a demon-possessed woman who many believe earned her living as a prostitute. She met Jesus, he delivered her, and she along with other women devoted their resources to supporting his earthly ministry. Mary Magdalene was there for the good times and the bad.

When they arrested Jesus in the garden of Gethsemane, the disciples all ran. Peter denied Jesus three times. As far as we know, the only disciple who followed Jesus from arrest to crucifixion was John. But we do know the women stuck with him the whole time. Their loyalty never wavered. And we know that only one woman—Mary Magdalene, for reasons I can only speculate about—went to the tomb that morning.

Even after Jesus was dead, even after it appeared all hope was lost and that the miracle worker, the Messiah, would no longer walk among them, Mary still went.

And Jesus rewarded that loyalty. Even though Peter and John went to the tomb later, they saw no angels; they didn't see Jesus. In fact, look at what they did see and do when they reached the tomb.

Peter therefore went out, and the other disciple, and were going to the tomb. So they both ran together, and the other disciple outran Peter and came to the tomb first. And he, stooping down and looking in, saw the linen cloths lying *there;* yet he did not go in. Then Simon Peter came, following him, and went into the tomb; and he saw the linen cloths lying *there,* and the handkerchief that had been around His head, not lying with the linen cloths, but folded together in a place by itself. Then the other disciple, who came to the tomb first, went in also; and he saw and believed. For as yet they did not know the Scripture, that He must rise again from the dead. Then the disciples went away again to their own homes. (John 20:3–10)

They went home. I wonder if the conversation between Peter and John went something like this:

JOHN: Peter, the woman's right; his body is gone.
PETER: Sure looks like it.
JOHN: What do you think happened?
PETER: I'm not sure.
JOHN: What do you think we should do?
PETER: I guess we just go home.

Just go home. After all Jesus taught them, after all the miracles he performed in front of them, it never occurred to these two guys something spectacular had happened. They didn't even feel as though they should maybe stick around and look for clues as to what happened.

Mary stuck around, if only to weep. Losing Jesus had devastated her. This man meant everything to her, and she was in no hurry to leave the last place his body had been. Jesus rewarded that loyalty.

For all history from now to eternity there will be one undeniable fact: The first human being to learn that Jesus Christ had risen was a woman. And not just any woman, but a former demon-possessed prostitute.

I want to put Mary Magdalene's social status into perspective.

In the city of Vancouver, British Columbia, prostitutes were going missing. Not all at once, mind you—just every now and then. Unlike the TV portrayal of prostitutes as glamorous women with hearts of gold, the word *pathetic* couldn't even adequately explain these prostitutes' lives.

Many of these women were abused as children. They turned to drugs and alcohol to deal with the abuse, then to prostitution to pay for the drugs and alcohol. They were burned-out drug addicts who sold all they had in order to survive.

They were to be pitied, but instead they were ignored. The police were aware some had disappeared but kept no real track of it. They just assumed the girls had moved on to another jurisdiction. Then some suspicious activity at a farm got the attention of the police. They now believe that over a twenty-two-year period, one man murdered sixty-one women. He's been officially charged with twenty-seven counts of murder.[1]

Mary Magdalene was that kind of woman. Her demon possession would be much like drug addiction. She would be living on the streets, and if she suddenly disappeared, no one would care.

I think Jesus deliberately chose the most marginalized woman in that society to reveal himself to after his resurrection. I think he did it so we'd never doubt how much he cares about women and how they're treated.

Anytime anyone gets it in their mind that women don't play a valuable role in the church, they should go back and think about that passage. The guys split; the girl stayed. It was the girl who God met after his resurrection, not the guys.

Just as when Jesus took the time to heal the woman who suffered from constant bleeding—something that his disciples would have thought hardly worth his attention—he took the time to let Mary know he was alive before he ascended to his Father.

Think about that for a moment. Jesus hadn't ascended to his Father yet. It's not inconceivable that the only reason he hadn't ascended yet was for Mary's sake; to reward her loyalty; to ease the grief of her suffering.

The beauty of loyalty to God is he always rewards it. Anything done for him out of a true spirit will be remembered. It's not so in this world, where loyalty is usually bought and often betrayed.

I once had a job as a woodlands accountant. Woodlands has a nice ring to it. It invokes images of someone managing the forest and making sure all the forest critters are safe and sound. In reality, I was the accountant who tracked how much it cost to log the forest and made sure everyone got paid. Woodlands just sounds nicer than logging accountant does.

In most companies woodlands accountants report to the controller, but it's not unusual for them to be loyal to the woodlands manager. He's the guy who actually runs the logging operations.

So, at that particular company I became loyal to the woodlands manager. One reason was because I liked him, and the other is I didn't particularly care for the controller.

It wasn't exactly the greatest place to work. It was a new mill; it had many start-up issues and cash-flow problems. Whenever money is tight in an organization, there are lots of problems.

One day, the woodlands manager was complaining to me that the controller was slow in paying logging contractors, and this was causing problems getting logs to the mill.

Since I had no love for the controller and cared more about how the logging went, I let him in on a little secret. I was none too delicate about it. The conversation went something like this:

"She's an idiot," I said.

"How so?" he asked.

"We've got over a million dollars coming to us from the federal government. All we've got to do is get our bookkeeping up-to-date and fill out a simple return, and they'll send us a check."

"Then why haven't we?" he said.

I laughed. "She's waiting for a computerized

accounting system a friend of hers designed before we can enter any transactions. Until then, we can't file the return."

"How long is that going to take?"

"We've been waiting a month so far," I said.

"Do we have to use that system?"

"No. There are other programs out there that cost less and would do just as good a job."

"So I can't pay my contractors because she won't use another system?"

"That's about it," I said.

So do you know what happened? He met with the controller and the company president. They had a huge yelling match where he blurted out to the controller in the president's presence that she was an idiot. Of course, he had to back up that particular remark.

He backed it up with everything I said and made sure they knew I'd said it.

So, the controller met with me later that day and announced the company really couldn't afford a woodlands accountant, but they did have an accounting clerk position available. In other words, I was fired.

So much for loyalty. I hadn't meant for him to repeat what I'd told him, but he did anyway. He saved his skin by sacrificing mine.

That's the wonderful thing about Jesus. He's completely loyal to us even when we're not so loyal to him. We never have to worry about him ratting us out. We don't have to worry that Jesus will pretend he never knew us when we get to heaven. Not only will he know us, but he'll welcome us into his kingdom.

Mary Magdalene understood more about Jesus than most people did. She knew that being loyal to Jesus wasn't a risk; it was a sure thing. Being loyal to family and friends in this world is a good thing, but it's not the kind of loyalty you place your faith in. People will betray you, sometimes by intent, sometimes by accident.

Jesus will never betray us. He has already made the first move. He showed us his loyalty when he went to that cross to pay for our sins. Don't think for a second he had to stay there. Jesus could have left that cross at any time. With a word, he could have ended it all right then and there. There would've been a flash of light, the crowd and the soldiers would've been dead, and Jesus would've been back in heaven safe with the angels.

He didn't do that because he made a promise to us. In the garden of Eden, God said,

> So the LORD God said to the serpent:
>   "Because you have done this,
>   You *are* cursed more than all cattle,
>   And more than every beast of the field;
>   On your belly you shall go,
>   And you shall eat dust
>   All the days of your life.
>   And I will put enmity
>   Between you and the woman,
>   And between your seed and her Seed;
>   He shall bruise your head,

And you shall bruise His heel." (Gen.
3:14–15)

God made it clear he was coming back—and then
he did. Jesus was born of Mary, and he bruised the ser-
pent's head. He defeated death and sin. He kept his
promise; he'll always keep his promises.

AFTERWORD

In reading this book, you may have come to the mistaken conclusion that a guy like this author must be the perfect man because he understands!

Sorry, I'm just as flawed as all the other men are. Feel free to ask my wife, my daughter, my mother, and the women who work for me at the office.

But there is one message I want to be sure you got from this book. You are not flawed. Our society has placed so much emphasis on physical perfection and occupational perfection. The women presented in the media look good, and they've usually got "power" jobs.

First of all, no one looks that good. To look that good requires professional hair and makeup—and possibly surgery. On top of that, you'd need flattering camera angles and postproduction touch-ups. The world has presented an illusion and told all women that's what they have to aspire to.

Second, there just aren't that many high-powered jobs out there. Someone has to work at take-out. Someone has to be the clerk in the office. Someone has to look after the kids. If we could all get high-powered jobs, who'd smile at us every morning when we get our expensive coffee? Would we be more valuable than they? In this world—yes. In God's world—no.

Am I saying you shouldn't try to look nice? Absolutely not. God went to a lot of trouble to create our bodies, and we should care for them. Am I saying you shouldn't try to better your occupation? Absolutely not. We should strive to use to the maximum the gifts God has given to us.

But what I am saying is this: Don't fall for this world's lie. Your value doesn't come from what this world thinks of you, it comes from what Jesus thinks of you. So when you're feeling down because you aren't all you're expected to be, just think of all the times God met a girl.

Think of how he treated them. That's how he plans on treating you—with unconditional love. A love so unconditional that he went to a cross just to redeem you to himself. Now if that doesn't make you feel worthwhile, I don't know what will.

I'd really appreciate hearing from you. You can

find my e-mail address at the Web site for this book, www.godmetagirl.com.

READERS' GUIDE

For

Personal Reflection

or

Group Discussion

I pray that this book has touched you with the power of those moments when God met a girl. Those events touched lives then and continue to touch lives today. With that in mind, I realize some readers may be left with a desire to understand some truths I've shared more fully. I've written this readers' guide to help you dig deeper into the chapters and Scriptures they're based on. I've also written it to challenge you to think about the world you now live in versus the one you will live in.

Take this opportunity to learn more about Jesus and yourself. Use it to help you grow in him and gain the confidence that comes from being in his love.

1: A WOMAN CAUGHT IN ADULTERY (GRACE)

Scripture reference: John 8:1–12

In this chapter, we read about a woman who deserved to be stoned to death according to the law of the day. We saw a group of men who would kill this woman—not so much because of what she did but because it would help further their political agenda of exposing Christ as a fraud. We saw a man who not only put the men to shame, but also extended grace to a woman who thought she was about to die.

I can think of two times in my life when

another person extended grace to me. One time was after an exam at college. At the next class, the instructor asked me to drop by his office afterward.

With the usual trepidation that comes with a summons to the instructor's office with no idea of why, I showed up. He had my unmarked paper on his desk.

He said to me, "Did you have any problems during the exam?"

I thought, *Where's he going with this?* "Other than fighting the flu, no."

He nodded his head. "That explains it. You missed a whole page." He handed the exam to me.

I couldn't believe it. I really did forget to answer a whole page. I felt sick. I was in the running for a scholarship and the race was tight. I just shook my head.

He said, "Answer it now," and handed me a pen.

The instructor had nothing to gain by helping me. He was well within his rights to mark the whole page wrong but chose not to. Like our sovereign Lord Jesus, he cut me a break just because he could. That's what grace is all about.

The other time I experienced grace was when a female police officer gave me a warning instead of a speeding ticket. Who says it doesn't pay to be a guy sometimes?

1. In this Bible passage, the men condemned Grace because of what she was and
because her doing it would serve their purposes.
Have you ever condemned a person based on
nothing more than who or what they were?

2. There are usually three reasons to condemn a person: You can make yourself look
better, you can make someone else you care for
look better, or it's fair and just to condemn this
person because they've harmed you or a loved
one. Try to think of an example of each from
your own life, then ask yourself—did I handle
that situation the way Jesus would?

3. Try to be as honest as you can with this one. You've just had a complete makeover at La Chez Nouveau Vous (in English that's "The New You Place"—just sounds more glamorous in French). This makeover cost a fortune, and both you and Natasha the stylist think it's great. You get home and your loved one is evasive. Do you want the truth or not? If you get the truth, are you able to accept it without condemning the bringer of truth?

4. Think back to when you were a teenager—or maybe you're a teenager now. Think of a time when you did something that disappointed your parents so much it almost broke their hearts. What was the one thing you wanted from them most—besides a big hug?

5. Now think of your own child or, if you don't have children, think of a niece or nephew about whom you care deeply. Imagine if they did something that disappointed you so much it broke your heart. Would you hold back a hug? Would you hold back forgiveness? If you answered the way I think you did, keep this in mind—neither would Jesus.

2: A Woman with an Issue of Blood (Faith)

Scripture reference: Mark 5:25–34

In this chapter, we read about a woman who suffered from constant, menstrual-like bleeding. Having lived in a home with two women for the past twenty-two years, I have some understanding what three to five days of this can do to a woman. But twelve years of nonstop cramps and bleeding—that's got to be unbearable. I'm astounded that Jesus made a point of healing this woman, and I'm astounded she managed to find the faith to try one more time.

1. Have you ever asked God for something and didn't get it? Why do you think that was? Was it a lack of faith, or did you ask for the wrong thing?

2. Faith is really another word for trust. If you trust someone, you believe they will act in your best interests. Think of ways you build trust with other people. Can you build faith with God using the same methods?

3. If you ask a well-trusted friend to do something for you, and they don't, does that mean they aren't your friend anymore, or does it mean they had a reason for what they did? Apply the same idea when you ask God for something and don't get it. Does that mean you shouldn't have faith in him anymore?

4. Every person suffers illness at one time or another and in differing degrees. Certainly, God still heals today, and faith is a key component of healing, but if healing doesn't come, how does faith help with suffering?

5. Some people are desirable to be around—some, like the woman with the issue of blood, are not. If Jesus allowed an unclean woman to touch him, what does that say our attitude should be toward the undesirable?

3: Bad Day to Be a Demon (Delivered)

Scripture reference: Luke 8:1–3

This chapter looked at Mary called Magdalene. All we really know about her past is she was demon possessed, and Jesus took care of that problem for her. From that point on, Mary spent her time caring for Jesus and his followers. She went from a social outcast to a servant of the Son of God. We can learn a lot from her.

1. Do you define your importance in society based on what you do for a living?

2. If what we do defines our worth, what happens when we can no longer do it? Do we become pointless?

3. Many people are seeking the meaning of life. Jesus said: "I am the way, the truth, and the life. No one comes to the Father except through Me" (John 14:6). Why aren't we satisfied knowing Jesus' love for us is what gives us meaning?

4. Looking again at the Bible verse in question 3, Jesus makes it clear he's the only way to God. If we aren't living for Jesus, where exactly are we trying to get to when we die?

5. Imagine you just got out of bed and you have to be at work soon. You work in a place where the boss constantly puts you down, your coworkers don't like you, the pay is lousy, and you have no prospects for a better job. On the way to the bus you run into Jesus and he asks you to do him a favor—he asks you to show his love to the people you work with until he can find you something better. Would that help you endure the job? Why or why not? Whom do you really work for?

4: OFF THE TRACKS (SLAMMED)

Scripture reference: Luke 10:38–42

This chapter looked at Jesus' visit to Martha's house. Two women took two completely different approaches. Mary saw an opportunity to sit at Jesus' feet; Martha saw an opportunity to give weary travelers a great meal. Martha let her social obligations slam her off the track of learning from Jesus.

1. If you're like me, it doesn't take much to knock you off the tracks when it comes to accomplishing what needs to be done in your day. What do you think is the one thing you could change to make sure you spend time with God each day?

2. If you had a choice (try to be honest about this), what would you rather do: spend two hours a week practicing as a member of the church choir, or spend two weeks in prayer meetings?

3. If you're anything like me, you picked choir in question 2. If you did, why do we tend to prefer ministries like choir over prayer when Jesus clearly commands us in the Bible to pray but doesn't tell us to join the choir? (By the way, I think choir is a wonderful ministry. I'm only using it as an example here, so no offense intended to choir members everywhere.)

4. It's Sunday morning, and you've hit the snooze button ten times too many and now you have five minutes to get ready for church. You have barely enough time to brush your hair, never mind applying makeup. Would you go to church as you are or let the circumstances of the morning prevent you from going?

5. How many times do you press the snooze button when you need to catch a plane? Why are we more worried about missing a flight than missing church?

6. Do you ever find yourself looking at what other people have and wishing you had better things as well? Considering we're only passing through this world and are only "strangers and pilgrims on the earth" (Heb. 11:13), why do we worry so much about what we have and what we do for a living here?

5: THE WOMAN AT THE WELL (THIRST)

Scripture reference: John 4:4–42

This chapter dealt with the woman I called Abigail, who was thirsty enough to listen to Jesus' words about living water. She drank of that water, then went and told her people about it. Jesus used Abigail to bring light to the Samaritans.

1. Why can we be so excited that we lose sleep the night before a trip to, say, Hawaii, but have a hard time dragging ourselves out of bed to go to church?

2. Why do you think the woman at the well had so many husbands and was currently living with another man? Why do some women just keep marrying the wrong type of guy?

3. To put the woman at the well in context, if you are not African American, imagine you are. Now imagine you're living in the inner city and the only thing white people have ever done is buy drugs in your neighborhood. You just bought two bottles of Pepsi. A white guy steps out of a nice car and says, "Hey, I'm really thirsty. Can I have one of those?" Would you give him one? Why or why not?

4. Now assume you gave him the bottle of Pepsi, he drained it in less than a minute, said thanks, gave you a thousand dollars for your kindness, got in the car, and left. Would you tell everyone you knew about the crazy white guy who gave you a thousand dollars for a Pepsi? Change it to instead of giving you a thousand dollars, he gave you a gospel tract and told you your neighbors need to know about Jesus, then left. Would you be just as willing to tell everyone about the crazy white guy who told you about Jesus?

WHEN GOD MET A GIRL

5. I'm convinced the woman at the well was God's chosen instrument to reach the Samaritans. What does that tell you about the importance of women in God's great plan for reaching the world?

6: A Boy Comes Back (Surprise)

Scripture reference: Luke 7:11–17

A widow lost her only son. And Jesus, just because he felt sorry for her, raised her son from the dead. Sometimes God does things for us just because he wants to. He's no different to us than we are to our children. We love them unconditionally and nurture and care for them because we want to. When we feel sorry for them, when they've been knocked down, we want to help them get back up again. So does he.

1. If you're old enough to read this book, you've probably experienced some kind of tragedy in your life. If you're a teenager, it might be something painful, such as breaking up or not getting asked out or the loss of a close family member. If you're older, I'm sure you've had

some life experience that wasn't all peaches and cream. In the darkest moments, did you pray to God for help? Did you blame him? Did you thank him and ask him to reveal his plan in his time?

2. Jesus healed the widow of Nain's son. Other women lost their sons or daughters, but he didn't raise them from the dead. This event seems almost to be a random act of compassion. How do you feel when you know God has healed others but hasn't healed you or a sick loved one?

3. If God has chosen not to bring healing in your situation, why do you think he has done that? Is it for your benefit, the benefit of others, or maybe something else?

4. There's something powerful and touching about the raising of the widow of Nain's son— other than the dead coming back to life. She had few or no resources to repay Jesus, and he didn't expect repayment. What message did his choosing to bless this particular woman send to the society in general?

5. Jesus was a constant symphony of surprises during his short ministry. He raised the dead, healed the sick, gave sight to the blind, and—most of all—gave hope. He really shook things up. Does he surprise us today? Has he ever surprised you?

7: AN UNUSUAL DINNER GUEST (BLINDNESS)

Scripture reference: Luke 7:36–50

We were both teenagers. We'd polished off at least a case of beer between us and were now driving down a main street in my friend's Camaro. The traffic light in the distance turned yellow, and my friend floored it. With alcohol-induced bravery, we whooped it up as he blew through the intersection at eighty miles an hour.

Thirty years have elapsed since that event. I still get prickles on the back of my neck when I think what could have happened. A second more and we could've plowed into another vehicle and ended up on the nightly news as two dead teenagers who killed or maimed a family on their way home from the movies.

It could have all been over thirty years ago. Thirty years ago, I could've met God without Jesus at my side.

In this chapter, we read about the bizarre incident of a woman of ill repute washing the Son of God's feet with her tears, drying them with her hair, and anointing him with perfume. Let's face it—if that happened in your church to your pastor, there would definitely be a board meeting.

But it didn't happen to your pastor. It happened to Jesus, and God made sure this event was recorded so we would know our sin and what we escaped. He wanted to make sure we understood that we've been forgiven much, and we should love much.

1. Two holidays in the year mark the death of those who fought and died for us—Veterans Day (Remembrance Day in Canada) and Good Friday. Which holiday gets the most airtime in the media? Why do you think that is?

2. Why do we find it easier to express our gratitude to armed-services personnel who defend our country than to the one who saved us for all eternity?

3. Why do you think it is that the greater the sinner we were (are), the more love we feel for Jesus when we accept his grace and salvation?

4. Recently in Vancouver, B.C., a truck went into the river. The woman who was driving the truck got out, but a policeman had to jump in and help her to shore. The media called him a hero; the policeman called the woman a hero for fighting so hard to get out of the truck and staying afloat in the river. Is there anything we can do to help save ourselves spiritually? Who is our hero?

5. It's a fact that a person can be the vilest offender and Jesus will extend grace and salvation to that person if they ask (Rom. 5:6–11). Think of the most horrible person—alive or dead—that comes to your mind. How does it make you feel knowing that if that person accepted Christ before death, they will spend eternity with Jesus and, presumably, you? Now, think of the worst thing you've ever done. Isn't it reasonable to assume that if he can forgive the most horrible person, he can forgive you?

8: THE LAST RESORT (DESPERATION)

Scripture reference: Matt. 15:21–28

In this chapter, we read about a Canaanite woman with a demon-possessed daughter. Even worse, the only person around who had a track record for casting out demons was a Jewish prophet. The Jews hated Canaanites. But this woman wouldn't let anything stop her from getting to Jesus and getting her daughter healed.

1. I talked about desperation as a way for God to get us where we need to go. Why can't we just go where we should be? Why is it necessary for God to use circumstances and events to get us there? Do you like it when he uses desperation to herd you?

2. Demon-possessed children are pretty rare in the Western world. Tragically, what isn't rare is children caught up in gangs, drugs, sex, and well, you name it. If your child is (or was) involved in a destructive lifestyle, would you love him or her less?

3. It's not unusual for parents to feel guilty when their children go offtrack to a lifestyle that's harmful to them. There's plenty of recrimination of what you could have done differently, but the fact is the outside world sometimes has more influence on children than the parents do. Is it appropriate to feel guilty when you've done all a parent can?

4. Let's say you decide to pray for your child since everything else you've tried has failed. You pray so much that the angels have taken to turning up the volume on their MP3 players to shut you out. How do you feel about the fact that after God hears your prayers, he may use tough circumstances of desperation to whack your child upside the head and bring him or her to his or her senses?

5. Think back to your answers in question 1 above and in chapter 4. Were your feelings about God using desperation to get you where he needs you to go different about your feelings about God using desperation to get your child to where they need to go?

9: YOU ARE OF GREAT VALUE (NOBODIES)

Scripture reference: Luke 13:10–17

This chapter talked about a woman who spent eighteen years crippled, until Jesus decided to make a point by healing her on the Sabbath. A lot of people use this passage to teach that anytime is a good time to do good works. I think there's more to it than that. The King of Heaven took the time to restore a marginalized person to health. He thumbed it in the establishment's face that no one was too low for him to love.

I think this chapter might have the most important message of all in this book. This world doesn't define our worth; our relationship with Jesus defines our worth. That makes us all pretty valuable.

1. Have you ever heard the saying "keeping up with the Joneses"? It refers to the practice of making sure you have what everyone else in your social class has. Who should we really be trying to keep up with?

2. Go to a mirror and take a look. Do you like what you see? If you do, how long do you think it will last before age catches up on you? If you don't, why don't you? Jesus likes what he sees.

3. Think about what you do for a living. Do you have a job that commands a good wage and respect in the community? If so, will you be able to keep that job for eternity? If you have a menial job that pays poorly, will you have that job for eternity?

4. Look at your home. Is it the envy of the neighborhood? Will you live there for eternity? Is your home humble? Will you have to live there for eternity?

5. If Jesus Christ is the Son of God and died on a cross because he loved you so much, then why do you care about how you look, where you work, where you live? You're only going to be on this planet for a blip of time compared to eternity; whose opinion should you really care about?

6. Have you ever played Monopoly? Think about how valuable that paper money and those paper deeds are while the game is on. What value do those things hold once the game ends? Can we draw a parallel from this and apply it to the world we live in?

10: I'LL GET THERE WHEN I GET THERE (POWER)

Scripture reference: John 11:1–44

In this chapter, we learned about one of history's greatest miracles. Jesus raised a man from the dead whose body was stone-cold gone. He did it to show all of us his unlimited power. He did it to show he cares for his friends. Martha, Mary, and Lazarus were Jesus' friends. He didn't come when they wanted him to, but he came when they needed him to.

1. Everyone has power over someone: bosses over workers, parents over children, children over family pets. What kind of power do you have? Do you use it for your good, or others' good?

2. You probably remember from your childhood a kid saying, "My dad can beat up your dad." Who is your real father? Is there anyone who can beat him up?

3. There are two types of management styles. In one style, you rule over your workers, making all the decisions and making it clear they aren't to think for themselves. In the other, you empower the people who work for you, teaching them how to make good decisions and giving them the tools to do their job. Which method do you think is better? Which one does God use?

4. In theory, the government has the power to rule over us. They make laws that dictate how we behave—yet we don't behave, thus there are jails. This means the government's power is _____. If you want to change society, can it best be changed by laws? What method did Jesus use to change his society?

5. It's always sad to see someone who has retired return to their place of work and realize that yesterday they were the boss and today they're a guest. If we truly serve God, will that ever happen to us?

11: UNEXPECTED ALLY (COURAGE)

Scripture reference: Matt. 27:19

In this chapter, we looked at the dream of Claudia Procola, Pontius Pilate's wife. I debated whether or not to include this incident. Not all commentators agree on whether the dream was from God. However, Matthew Henry (probably one of the most respected commentators of all time) did, and the text of his comments can be found in the endnote.[1]

1. Do you think Claudia's dream came from God? If it didn't come from God, where did it come from? Keep in mind Claudia learned in this dream Jesus was a "just Man."

2. Is courage always a good thing? Currently there's a TV show where contestants perform dangerous stunts. Performing these stunts takes courage, but does anything good really come from this courage?

3. Referring back to question 2: These stunts on television are performed with plenty of safeguards to prevent the participants' death or injury. Is it real courage when the participant has a "safety net"? Compare this to a SWAT unit (Special Weapons and Tactics, a specialized police unit that handles dangerous situations) that has to charge into a building of gunmen holding hostages. Is their courage the same as the TV-show participants'?

4. Imagine you work for a bank. Your boss has just told you to cash a check for a friend of hers and ignore normal procedures. You know the bank policy doesn't allow this. Would you have enough courage to say no to her? Now, think of that same boss in a different situation. She's just told you her life is coming down all around her. Would you be able to tell her about Jesus?

5. Generally speaking, we have more courage sticking up for our rights than we do telling people about Jesus. Why do you think that is?

6. In question 3, I mentioned the TV-show participants have a safety net. When Jesus went to the cross to die, do you think he knew what dying felt like? If you knew what dying felt like, would it make it any easier?

7. We live in high-stress world. All our technology has only served to make life more complex, not simpler. It seems almost daily now there's a natural disaster or a foreign threat. It's a scary world. How can knowing the Scriptures give you the courage to face the world's daily struggles?

12: Everything Has Changed (Loyalty)

Scripture reference: John 19:1—20:18

In this chapter, we looked at Jesus' trial and crucifixion through Mary Magdalene's eyes. We then moved on to the glorious events surrounding the empty tomb.

1. Why do you think Mary went to the tomb that morning? Do you think she thought Jesus was alive, or did she just want to check on the body?

2. When you think of all Jesus did, why do
you think Mary was the only one going to the
body? Why didn't more people care about what
happened to his body after he died?

3. Mary showed loyalty beyond what anyone
could expect. Do you think her level of loyalty
might relate to how much Jesus did for her
when he delivered her from demons and the life
she led?

4. As an accountant, I have a favorite saying: "Only those you trust can betray you, so only those you trust can steal from your company." The reasoning is simple: You don't give those you don't trust any opportunity to betray you. Mary didn't betray Jesus, but others who claimed to love him—such as Peter—did. Why do you think Peter denied Jesus? Would you have done differently?

5. On the cross, Jesus said, "It is finished." What was finished; his life, or something more important?

NOTES

2: A Woman with an Issue of Blood (Faith)

1. The laws related to this woman's uncleanness are covered in Leviticus 15:19–30. The law doesn't require her to live separately from the other people; however, anyone touching her becomes unclean. Compare this to Leviticus 13:45–46 that requires lepers to live outside the camp.

4: Off the Tracks (Slammed)

1. Kim Hauenstein, "Mary and Martha," http://www.upcam.org/MaryMartha.htm (accessed September 13, 2006).

5: The Woman at the Well (Thirst)

1. Craig A. Evans, ed., *The Bible Knowledge Commentary/New Testament* (Colorado Springs: Cook Communications Ministries, 2000), 284.

2. This is a paraphrase of a joke where a rich white woman has a black maid. When she dies, the rich white woman finds her reward in heaven is a cottage, and the black maid's reward is a mansion. She asks why the disparity, and the angel tells the white woman, "We did the best we could with what you sent on ahead." The point is what we see as unworthy people on earth are worthy people in heaven.

7: An Unusual Dinner Guest (Blindness)

1. Craig A. Evans, ed., *The Bible Knowledge Commentary/New Testament* (Colorado Springs: Cook Communications Ministries, 2000), 223.

11: Unexpected Ally (Courage)

1. Pastor Nicholas Brie, Trinity Evangelical Lutheran Church, Taneytown, MD. "Pilate's Wife," http://www.emmitsburg.net/tlc/pastor_brie/2004/pilates_wife.htm.

12: Everything Has Changed (Loyalty)

1. CBC News Online, "The Missing Women of Vancouver," March 2, 2006, http://www.cbc.ca/news/background/pickton/.

FROM READERS' GUIDE QUESTIONS FOR CHAPTER 11

1. The tenderness and care of Pilate's wife, in sending this caution, thereupon, to her husband; *Have nothing to do with that just man.* First, this was an honourable testimony to our Lord Jesus, witnessing for him that he was a *just man,* even then when he was persecuted as the worst of malefactors: when his friends were afraid to appear in defence of him, God made even those that were strangers and enemies, to speak in his favour; when Peter denied him, Judas confessed him; when the chief priests pronounced him guilty of death, Pilate declared he *found no fault* in him; when the women that loved him stood afar off, Pilate's wife, who knew little of him, showed a concern for him. Note, God will not leave himself without witnesses to the truth and equity of his cause, even when it seems to be most spitefully run down by its enemies, and most shamefully deserted by its friends. *Second,* It was a fair warning to Pilate; *Have nothing to do with him.* Note: God has many ways of giving checks to sinners in their sinful pursuits, and it is a great mercy to have such checks from Providence, from faithful friends, and from our own consciences; it is also our great duty to hearken to them. *O do not this abominable thing which the Lord hates,* is what we may hear said to us, when we are entering into temptation, if we will but regard it. Pilate's lady sent him this warning, out of

the love she had to him; she feared not a rebuke from him for meddling with that which belonged not to her; but, let him take it how he would, she would give him the caution. Note, It is an instance of true love to our friends and relations, to do what we can to keep them from sin; and the nearer any are to us, and the greater affection we have for them, the more solicitous we should be not to suffer sin to come or lie upon them, Leviticus 19:17. The best friendship is friendship to the soul. We are not told how Pilate turned this off, probably with a jest; but by his proceeding against the just man it appears that he did not regard it. Thus faithful admonitions are made light of, when they are given as warnings against sin, but will not be so easily made light of, when they shall be reflected upon as aggravations of sin. (Taken from Matthew Henry, *Commentary on the Whole Bible* [Grand Rapids: Zondervan, 1963], 1351.)

ABOUT THE AUTHOR

Andrew Snaden is an accountant who lives in Prince George, British Columbia, with his wife of twenty-five years. The area truly has four seasons, and Snaden enjoys golf in the summer, and hockey and skiing in the winter. He has written or cowritten three full-length novels; this is his first nonfiction work. You can find more information at his Web site, www.godmetagirl.com. He enjoys receiving e-mails from readers.

Additional copies of *When God Met a Girl*
are available wherever good books are sold.

If you have enjoyed this book,
or if it has had an impact on your life,
we would like to hear from you.

Please contact us at

LIFE JOURNEY
Cook Communications Ministries, Dept. 201
4050 Lee Vance View
Colorado Springs, CO 80918

Or visit our Web site
www.cookministries.com

LIFE JOURNEY®
Bringing Home the Message for Life